Always Delicious

Low-FODMAP Kitchen

Always Delicious

Low-FODMAP Kitchen

100+ stress-free
lunches and dinners
to manage food
intolerances and IBS

Chrissy Glentis

murdoch books

Sydney | London

Contents

Introduction

Welcome to the *Always Delicious Low-FODMAP Kitchen*.

If you're holding this book, chances are you've heard of the low-FODMAP diet and its potential to improve digestive health, especially for those with irritable bowel syndrome (IBS) and other functional gastrointestinal disorders. This cookbook is designed to make your journey with the low-FODMAP diet not only manageable but enjoyable. Here, you'll find a collection of simple, easy-to-follow recipes that will help you navigate your way to stress-free cooking.

What is the low-FODMAP diet?

The low-FODMAP diet was developed by researchers at Monash University in Australia. FODMAPs are a group of short-chain carbohydrates and sugar alcohols found in various foods that can be difficult for some people to digest. These include:

Fermentable
Oligosaccharides (found in foods such as wheat, garlic and onion)
Disaccharides (found in foods such as milk, yoghurt and soft cheese)
Monosaccharides (found in foods such as apple, honey and
    high-fructose corn syrup)
And
Polyols (found in foods such as stone fruits and artificial sweeteners).

By reducing high-FODMAP foods, many people experience significant relief from symptoms such as bloating, gas, diarrhoea, constipation and abdominal pain. The low-FODMAP diet has also been shown to help manage the symptoms of endometriosis, ulcerative colitis and Crohn's disease.

I don't want to turn you off if you are beginning your journey into low-FODMAP eating, but it's no walk in the park. Those who have been on their journey for a few weeks, months or years will know exactly what I am talking about. It's hard to eat out, it's tough to figure out, and it can honestly be quite frustrating.

The goal of this cookbook

That's where this cookbook comes in. Here, I share recipes I have developed over the past decade, including some new ones, that I hope will re-ignite not only your joy of cooking but also eating.

The beauty of these recipes is that they are easy for anyone to make. I always endeavour to use as few ingredients as possible so you can make delicious food that is stress free both for your tummy and your mind! Quick and tasty is my motto. We all have busy lives, and we don't need to be slaving away in the kitchen just because we have intolerances or allergies.

My goal is to simplify the low-FODMAP diet for you and make following it a little bit less stressful. I believe that everyone deserves to enjoy delicious meals without the stress of complex recipes or hard-to-find ingredients. Each recipe in this book is crafted to be:

- **Simple:** Easy-to-follow instructions that require minimal effort and time
- **Accessible:** Ingredients that are readily available at your local supermarket
- **Tasty:** Flavoursome, to prove that eating low FODMAP can be delicious
- **Efficient:** Many recipes are designed with batch cooking in mind, allowing you to prepare meals in advance and save time during busy weekdays.

How do I know all of this?

Well, like you (or your loved one), I too need to follow a low-FODMAP diet. And, just like you, I was dismayed and frustrated by the lack of options and the difficulty around it all. So, ten years ago, my husband and I started our own business in Melbourne, Australia. My goal has always been to take the stress out of eating and to help people on a low-FODMAP diet enjoy food again – in all aspects: the eating, the cooking, the flavour.

Some of you may know me or have heard of our business, Foddies (a play on the term 'low FODMAP' that also serves as an inclusive adjective to encompass all of us on the diet – 'You're a Foddie like me!', 'We're all Foddies'). Over the past ten years, I have created hundreds of recipes that I have shared through our cafes, restaurants, packaged products and, during COVID, a fresh meal-delivery service. The focus has always been on making food that tastes so good no one will know it's low FODMAP, gluten free, dairy free and allergy friendly.

How to use this cookbook

Getting started

If you are just starting your journey on the low-FODMAP diet, then it is recommended you seek the assistance of a dietitian to help you determine your specific triggers, as this diet is not one size fits all. Having said that, this book is a great resource no matter your condition.

I have included a table with the key ingredients used in this cookbook and their low-FODMAP quantities (see page 14).

Cooking flexibly

Every recipe in this book is low FODMAP. The serving sizes are based on current information available at the time of writing this book. Many recipes are also dairy free, lactose free, egg free, nut free and soy free, and all can be made gluten free (if they aren't already). Keep an eye out for these icons:

DF dairy free   EF egg free   GF gluten free

LF lactose free   NF nut free   SF soy free

If a recipe can be easily adapted to suit any of these restrictions, you will see an outline rather than a solid colour.

Some ingredients, such as tomato sauce (ketchup), soy sauce, fish sauce and stock cubes, can contain gluten, so if you are gluten free, be sure to check the ingredients.

Everyone's tolerance to FODMAPs is different. Use this book as a guide and adjust the ingredients according to your personal tolerance levels. Basically, make these recipes your own by simply omitting or substituting ingredients suited to your specific needs.

Planning meals

When you see the icon below, you'll know that the recipe is perfect for meal prepping or batch cooking. Use these recipes to help structure your days and weeks. This will make it easier to stay on track and avoid high-FODMAP foods. I especially love having meals on hand in the freezer for those days when I can't be bothered to cook or when I need something quick to eat.

Following the recipes

- Low-FODMAP chicken or beef stock cubes can be substituted for Low-FODMAP chicken stock (page 217) or Low-FODMAP beef stock (page 215), or you can use store-bought alternatives. For example, if a recipe calls for two stock cubes and 400 ml (14 fl oz) water, you can substitute this with 400 ml (14 fl oz) chicken or beef stock and omit the water and stock cubes.
- Certain ingredients, such as pasta, bread and butter, can be substituted for dairy- or gluten-free alternatives fairly easily at a 1:1 ratio; flour, however, can be a little trickier (see the next point).
- All baking recipes are gluten free. If you can tolerate regular wheat flour or spelt flour, feel free to substitute with that, but the results may differ, as gluten-free flour needs more liquid than regular flour. So, if you are substituting, add the liquid slowly and prepare to use a little less. Xanthan gum acts a little bit like gluten, giving mixtures made with gluten-free flour elasticity and structure. It is not needed for recipes made with regular plain (all-purpose) flour, so please include or omit as required.
- Some of you may be wondering why garlic-infused olive oil is safe. Without getting too much into the science, the simple reason is that FODMAPs are water soluble, so when you're cooking with regular garlic, the FODMAPs leach into the food; but when garlic is added to oil, the flavour works its way into the oil, but the FODMAPs in the garlic are locked in place as they cannot permeate the oil. This results in flavour without the FODMAPs. The same goes for onion oil. However, please do not make this at home! Only use store-bought infused oils because bacteria grow in these oils if they're not manufactured correctly. This can result in botulism, a serious illness caused by toxins that attack the body's nerves.
- Similar to garlic oil, the FODMAPs in tinned legumes leach into the water inside the tin. This is why tinned legumes are lower in FODMAPs than fresh or dried varieties.

Many fruits and vegetables are only low FODMAP in certain amounts (an accurate pair of kitchen scales is a low-FODMAP must-have!). All of the recipes in this book have been formulated to be low FODMAP on a per-serve basis, but I think it's helpful to understand what quantities of certain ingredients are considered low-FODMAP more generally.

Key Ingredients:

What's Safe and What to Avoid

This table contains a breakdown of common ingredients and their low-FODMAP amounts. Use it as a reference and to double check portion sizes if needed. That said, my aim with this book is to take the stress out of eating, so I hope you don't feel compelled to keep referring back to it and can instead just dive in and enjoy cooking and eating!

As you progress in your low-FODMAP journey, you will determine which particular FODMAPs you react to and know if you can tolerate a little more of certain ingredients.

Ingredient	Low FODMAP (safe)
Almond	10 nuts (approx. 12 g)
Almond meal	⅓ cup (35 g)
Avocado	3 tablespoons (60 g/approx. ¼ avocado)
Banana	Firm: 95 g (3¼ oz/approx. 1 medium banana) Ripe: 37 g (1¼ oz/approx. ⅓ medium banana)
Beef stock	No onion or garlic
Butter	1 tablespoon (20 g/¾ oz)
Cabbage	Common/white: 75 g (2¾ oz) Red: 75 g (2¾ oz) Green/Savoy: 40 g (1½ oz)
Chicken stock	No onion or garlic
Chickpea	¼ cup (40 g) (tinned, drained and rinsed)
Chive	Up to 500 g (1 lb 2 oz)
Coconut milk	¼ cup (60 ml)
Corn	Fresh/frozen: 40 g (1½ oz) Creamed: ⅓ cup (100 g) Tinned: ½ cup (75 g)
Cranberry	2 tablespoons (approx. 20 g)
Edamame	½ cup (75 g)
Eggplant (aubergine)	1 cup (75 g)

Fennel	¾ cup (75 g)
Feta cheese	Up to 500 g (1 lb 2 oz)
Garlic	Garlic-infused olive oil (see page 10)
Green capsicum (pepper)	1 cup (75 g)
Kale	½ cup (75 g)
Leek	Green tops and leaves (white bulbs are not low FODMAP)
Lentil	¼ cup (46 g) (tinned, drained and rinsed)
Macadamia nut	15 nuts (approx. 30 g)
Olive	⅓ cup (60 g)
Pumpkin (squash)	Butternut: 63 g (2¼ oz) Kabocha (Japanese), Kent or Jarrahdale: 75 g (2¾ oz)
Raspberry	60 g (2 oz)
Red capsicum (pepper)	½ cup (43 g)
Rhubarb	1 cup (150 g)
Ricotta cheese	2 tablespoons (40 g)
Spring onion (scallion)	Green tops (white bulbs are not low FODMAP)
Strawberry	65 g (2½ oz)
Strawberry jam	2 tablespoons (40 g)
Sweet potato	½ cup (75 g)
Tomato	Common: 65 g (2½ oz) Cherry: 45 g (1¾ oz) Roma: 45 g (1¾ oz)
Tomato sauce (ketchup)	13 g (½ oz)
Walnut	15 halves (approx. 30 g)
Zucchini (courgette)	67 g (2½ oz)

In my opinion, soups are underrated. They're simple and flavoursome, and they're great not only in the winter months but also during summer as a lighter option. Not to mention they freeze well; I consider it mandatory to have a couple of soups in my freezer for meal prep or for when I'm feeling a little under the weather. Nothing warms the cockles like a bowl of nourishing soup!

These recipes are my take on some classics that are typically laden with onion, garlic and other high-FODMAP ingredients. By making some small tweaks here and there, you will be amazed that these classics are back on the menu.

Soup-erb

Comebacks

I had never had chowder, until I created this recipe during the COVID lockdowns in Melbourne. I was blown away by how delicious and easy it was and haven't looked back since! This creamy, rich soup is now a staple in our house, and I honestly don't know how I ever lived without it.

Bacon and potato chowder

Prep time: 15 minutes
Cook time: 30 minutes
Serves: 6

½ tablespoon garlic-infused
  olive oil
200 g (7 oz) bacon, diced
300 g (10½ oz) carrot, peeled
  and cut into bite-sized pieces
670 g (1 lb 8 oz) potato, peeled
  and cut into bite-sized pieces
1 teaspoon dried thyme
3 low-FODMAP chicken stock
  cubes (omit if using chicken
  stock)
¼ teaspoon salt
½ teaspoon black pepper
2⅔ cups (670 ml) water or
  Low-FODMAP chicken stock
  (page 217)
2⅔ cups (670 ml) lactose-free
  or dairy-free milk
140 g (5 oz) frozen or tinned
  corn kernels
2 tablespoons cornflour
  (cornstarch), mixed with
  ¼ cup (60 ml) water
  (see Tip)
fresh thyme sprigs, to garnish

Heat the garlic oil in a stockpot and sauté the bacon until it begins to brown, then add the carrot and sauté for another 3–4 minutes.

Add all the remaining ingredients, except the corn kernels and cornflour slurry, and bring to a simmer over medium heat. Cook for 15–20 minutes, or until the carrot and potato are cooked through.

Add the corn and cornflour slurry and stir until the chowder is thick and creamy, about 2–3 minutes.

Divide the soup between bowls and serve straight away, garnished with fresh thyme, or store in the fridge for 3–4 days or in portions in the freezer for up to 3 months.

For the best results, allow the frozen soup to thaw overnight in the fridge before heating in the microwave for 2–3 minutes, stirring halfway through until evenly heated. You can also reheat it from frozen in the microwave for 4–6 minutes. Add a little water, if necessary, to achieve your desired consistency.

Tip: The cornflour and water mixture should have the consistency of a slurry. If it's gluggy, whisk the mixture with a fork until there are no clumps of cornflour before adding it to the pot.

DF EF GF LF NF SF

You will love the depth of flavour in this quick, super-simple soup. By roasting the capsicum (pepper) in the oven, you get a lovely sweetness that complements the tomatoes and creates a beautiful umami-rich flavour.

Roasted capsicum and tomato soup

Prep time: 15–20 minutes
Cook time: 25 minutes
Serves: 6

4 red capsicums (peppers)
2 × 400 g (14 oz) tins tomatoes
3 teaspoons salt
1 teaspoon black pepper
3 teaspoons dried basil
2 teaspoons garlic-infused
    olive oil, plus extra for drizzling
3 teaspoons dried chives
fresh basil leaves, to garnish
    (optional)

Preheat the oven to 200°C (400°F).

Place the capsicums on a baking tray and roast until the skins have blackened, about 15–20 minutes. Keep an eye on them and turn halfway through.

Once the capsicums are ready, remove them from the oven, place in a heatproof bowl and cover with plastic wrap. The capsicums will start to sweat, which will allow the skins to be removed more easily. Leave to cool.

While the capsicum is cooling, add all the other ingredients to a stockpot with 4 cups (1 litre) water.

Once cooled, peel the blackened skin off the capsicums and remove the seeds and stalks, then add the flesh to the pot with the other ingredients and purée everything with a hand-held blender.

Place the pot over medium–high heat and bring to the boil. Turn the heat down to medium–low and simmer for 5–10 minutes to allow the flavours to develop, then remove from the heat and enjoy straight away, garnished with an extra drizzle of olive oil and some fresh basil leaves, if using. Alternatively, store in the fridge for 3–4 days or in portions in the freezer for up to 3 months.

For the best results, allow the frozen soup to thaw overnight in the fridge and heat in the microwave for 2–3 minutes, stirring halfway through, until evenly heated. You can also reheat it from frozen in the microwave for 4–6 minutes. Add a little water, if necessary, to achieve your desired consistency.

DF EF GF LF NF SF

Yes, you can have leek! Well, the top part anyway. You might be surprised to hear that you can get decent leek flavour from just the green tops. Don't believe me? Prepare to be converted!

Potato and leek soup

Prep time: 5 minutes
Cook time: 30 minutes
Serves: 4–6

⅓ cup (80 ml) garlic-infused olive oil

160 g (5¾ oz) leek tops, green part only, washed thoroughly and sliced

630 g (1 lb 3 oz) potato, peeled and cut into 3 cm (1¼ in) cubes

1¼ teaspoons dried thyme

1 teaspoon dried chives

2½ low-FODMAP chicken stock cubes

1 teaspoon salt

½ teaspoon black pepper

Heat the oil in a stockpot over medium–high heat and sauté the leek tops until softened, about 5–8 minutes. Add the potato and sauté for a further 2–3 minutes.

Add all the remaining ingredients with 1.7 litres (59 fl oz) water and bring to the boil. Once boiling, turn the heat down to low and simmer for 15–20 minutes until the potato can be easily pierced with a fork. Remove from the heat and blend with a hand-held blender, or transfer to an upright blender and blend until smooth.

Serve straight away or store in the fridge for 3–4 days or in portions in the freezer for up to 3 months.

For the best results, allow the frozen soup to thaw overnight in the fridge and heat in the microwave for 2–3 minutes, stirring halfway through, until evenly heated. You can also reheat it from frozen in the microwave for 4–6 minutes. Add a little water, if necessary, to achieve your desired consistency.

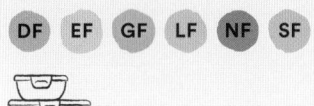

DF EF GF LF NF SF

If you don't have a pumpkin (squash) soup in your repertoire, then you definitely need to bookmark this recipe. Pumpkin soup is such a classic staple loved by everyone for its thick, creamy texture and oh-so-delicious flavour. I like to add carrot and sweet potato to help bulk up the quantity without overdoing it with high-FODMAP ingredients. Unfortunately, not all pumpkin is created equal. Kabocha (Japanese) or Kent are the lowest-FODMAP varieties of pumpkin but others, such as Jarrahdale, could also work. Just be sure to check the safe quantity (see page 15).

Pumpkin soup

Prep time: 10 minutes
Cook time: 30 minutes
Serves: 6

2 tablespoons garlic-infused
    olive oil
500 g (1 lb 2 oz) kabocha
    (Japanese) pumpkin (squash),
    skin removed, cut into 5 cm
    (2 in) dice
400 g (14 oz) carrot, peeled
    and cut into 5 cm (2 in) dice
300 g (10½ oz) sweet potato,
    peeled and cut into 5 cm
    (2 in) dice
1 teaspoon dried chives
½ teaspoon dried rosemary
1½ teaspoons salt
½ teaspoon black pepper
¼ teaspoon ground turmeric
10 cups (2.5 litres) water or
    Low-FODMAP chicken stock
    (page 217)
6 low-FODMAP chicken stock
    cubes (omit if using chicken
    stock)

Heat the garlic oil in a stockpot over medium–high heat and sauté the pumpkin, carrot and sweet potato for 5–10 minutes until it's beginning to soften.

Add all the remaining ingredients and bring to the boil over high heat. Once boiling, reduce the heat to low and simmer for 15–20 minutes until all the vegetables are soft when pierced with a fork.

Remove from the heat and carefully purée with a hand-held blender, or transfer to an upright blender and blitz until smooth.

Serve straight away or store in the fridge for 3–4 days or in portions in the freezer for up to 3 months.

For the best results, allow the frozen soup to thaw overnight in the fridge and heat in the microwave for 2–3 minutes, stirring halfway through, until evenly heated. You can also reheat it from frozen in the microwave for 4–6 minutes. Add a little water, if necessary, to achieve your desired consistency.

DF EF GF LF **NF** SF

Is there a more comforting soup than chicken noodle? While this is not 100 per cent traditional, the essence is still there and it is bound to bring back nostalgic memories of warming soup on winter days. Serve with crusty bread for maximum comfort.

Chicken noodle soup

Prep time: 10 minutes
Cook time: 20 minutes
Serves: 6

8 cups (2 litres) water or Low-FODMAP chicken stock (page 217)
5 low-FODMAP chicken stock cubes (omit if using chicken stock)
½ tablespoon garlic-infused olive oil
2 bay leaves
1 tablespoon dried chives
1 tablespoon dried parsley
½ teaspoon ground turmeric
300 g (10½ oz) skinless chicken breast, cut into 2 cm (¾ in) thick strips
190 g (6¾ oz) carrot, cut into 1 cm (½ in) dice
190 g (6¾ oz) zucchini (courgette), cut into 1 cm (½ in) dice
85 g (3 oz) vermicelli rice noodles
salt and black pepper, to taste

To a stockpot, add the water and stock cubes (or chicken stock), garlic oil, dried herbs and turmeric and bring to the boil, then reduce the heat to a simmer.

Add the chicken breast and poach in the liquid for 5 minutes, or until the chicken is cooked through and no longer pink. Transfer the chicken to a bowl.

Add the carrot and zucchini to the stock and simmer until softened, about 5–10 minutes.

While the vegetables are cooking, shred the cooked chicken, either by hand or in the bowl of a stand mixer fitted with the whisk attachment (start slow and increase the speed as needed). Return the shredded chicken to the pot and turn off the heat.

Break up the rice noodles into bite-sized pieces and add to the pot to cook in the residual heat. Once the noodles are cooked, after 3–5 minutes, season to taste with salt and pepper and allow to cool slightly before serving.

Serve straight away or store in the fridge for 3–4 days or in portions in the freezer for up to 3 months.

For the best results, allow the frozen soup to thaw overnight in the fridge and heat in the microwave for 2–3 minutes, stirring halfway through, until evenly heated. You can also reheat it from frozen in the microwave for 4–6 minutes. Add a little water, if necessary, to achieve your desired consistency.

Some ingredients are just made to go together, like chicken and sweetcorn. This take on the classic chicken and sweetcorn soup uses less corn than the original to keep it low FODMAP, but it still has enough sweetness to make your tastebuds sing.

Chicken and sweetcorn soup

Prep time: 5 minutes
Cook time: 20–25 minutes
Serves: 4

1 low-FODMAP chicken stock
   cube
250 g (9 oz) skinless chicken
   breast, cut into 2 cm (¾ oz)
   thick strips
1 × 420 g (15 oz) tin creamed
   corn
1 egg
½ tablespoon cornflour
   (cornstarch) mixed with
   2 tablespoons water (see Tip,
   page 20)
salt and black pepper, to taste
sesame oil, to taste

In a stockpot, combine 6 cups (1.5 litres) water with the stock cube and bring it to the boil over high heat.

Once the stock is boiling, reduce the heat to medium–low and add the chicken. Cook for 5–10 minutes, or until the chicken is no longer pink, then transfer to a bowl and either shred by hand or in a stand mixer fitted with the whisk attachment (start slow and increase the speed as needed).

Next, add the creamed corn to the pot with the shredded chicken.

Crack the egg into a bowl and whisk lightly to break up the yolk.

While the soup is simmering, pour in the beaten egg in a steady stream, stirring continuously. The egg should form lovely ribbons in the soup.

Finally, add the cornflour slurry and stir until the soup has thickened. Remove from the heat and season with salt, pepper and sesame oil to taste. Start slowly with the sesame oil, as it has a strong flavour.

Serve straight away or store in the fridge for 3–4 days or in portions in the freezer for up to 3 months.

For the best results, allow the frozen soup to thaw overnight in the fridge and heat in the microwave for 2–3 minutes, stirring halfway through, until evenly heated. You can also reheat it from frozen in the microwave for 4–6 minutes. Add a little water, if necessary, to achieve your desired consistency.

This classic soup has been reworked to remove the beans and other high-FODMAP ingredients, but the traditional flavour remains. It's a lovely, simple recipe that fills you up and warms the soul.

Minestrone soup

Prep time: 10 minutes
Cook time: 25 minutes
Serves: 4

1 tablespoon garlic-infused
   olive oil
160 g (5¾ oz) carrot, peeled
   and cut into bite-sized pieces
240 g (8½ oz) potato, peeled
   and cut into bite-sized pieces
160 g (5¾ oz) zucchini
   (courgette), cut into bite-sized
   pieces
2 low-FODMAP chicken stock
   cubes
200 g (7 oz) tinned tomatoes
1 tablespoon dried chives
1 teaspoon dried basil
80 g (2¾ oz) dried pasta of
   your choice
40 g (2¾oz) baby spinach
½ cup (110 g) tinned lentils,
   drained and rinsed (optional)
salt and black pepper, to taste

Heat the garlic oil in a stockpot over medium heat and sauté the carrot and potato for 2–3 minutes until beginning to soften.

Add all the other ingredients, except the pasta, spinach and lentils, with 4 cups (1 litre) water and bring to the boil over high heat. Turn the heat down to medium–low and simmer until the vegetables are cooked, about 15 minutes.

Add the pasta and continue to simmer for another 5 minutes, then turn off the heat. Add the spinach and lentils (if using) and cover the pot with the lid. The pasta will continue to cook in the residual heat.

Once the pasta is cooked to your liking and the spinach is wilted, check the consistency of the soup, adding a little more water if necessary to thin it out. Season with salt and pepper to taste. Serve straight away or store in the fridge for 3–4 days or in portions in the freezer for up to 3 months.

For the best results, allow the frozen soup to thaw overnight in the fridge and heat in the microwave for 2–3 minutes, stirring halfway through, until evenly heated. You can also reheat it from frozen in the microwave for 4–6 minutes. Add a little water, if necessary, to achieve your desired consistency.

DF EF GF LF SF

The hardest part of this recipe is making your own curry paste and even that is as easy as blitzing the ingredients in a blender! The best part about making the paste yourself is that it can be tailored to suit your preferences. If you prefer your laksa less spicy, add a little less paste, use fewer chillies in the paste, or leave them out altogether.

Prawn and chicken Thai green laksa

Prep time: 10 minutes
Cook time: 25 minutes
Serves: 4

2 tablespoons extra-virgin olive oil

4 cups (1 litres) water or Low-FODMAP chicken stock (page 217)

4 low-FODMAP chicken stock cubes (omit if using chicken stock)

2 × 400 ml (14 fl oz) tins coconut milk

½ teaspoon salt

2 boneless, skinless chicken thighs (300 g/10½ oz each)

400 g (14 oz) rice noodles

300 g (10½ oz) frozen or fresh raw prawns (shrimp), peeled, tails on (if frozen, defrost in the fridge overnight)

200 g (7 oz) bok choy

200 g (7 oz) bean shoots, to serve

Add all the ingredients for the paste to an upright blender and blend until smooth. You can also use a hand-held blender for this.

Heat the oil in a stockpot over medium heat and cook the curry paste for 1–2 minutes until fragrant. Add the water and stock cubes (or chicken stock), plus another 2 cups (500 ml) water and the coconut milk and salt and bring to the boil over high heat.

Add the chicken and reduce the heat to medium–low. Simmer for 10–15 minutes until the chicken is cooked through and no longer pink.

While the chicken is cooking, cook the rice noodles according to the packet instructions, then drain and refresh under cold water.

Once the chicken is cooked, remove it from the pot and either shred it by hand or in a stand mixer fitted with the whisk attachment (start slow and increase the speed as necessary).

Next, add the prawns to the pot and simmer for 3–4 minutes, or until they are cooked through and have turned pink.

Finally, add the bok choy and cook for 1–2 minutes, then taste the soup and adjust the seasoning if needed. To serve, portion the cooked noodles into bowls and ladle the soup on top. Top with the bean shoots and extra coriander leaves.

This soup can be stored in the fridge for 3–4 days or in portions in the freezer for up to 3 months.

For the best results, allow the frozen soup to thaw overnight in the fridge and heat in the microwave for 2–3 minutes, stirring halfway through, until evenly heated. You can also reheat it from frozen in the microwave for 4–6 minutes. Add a little water, if necessary, to achieve your desired consistency.

Paste

1–2 green chillies
½ teaspoon ground turmeric
½ teaspoon ground cumin
15 g (½ oz) spring onion
(scallion), green tops only
1 lemongrass stalk, finely sliced
1 tablespoon minced or crushed
ginger
5 macadamia nuts
1½ tablespoons garlic-infused
olive oil
1 tablespoon fish sauce
1 tablespoon extra-virgin olive oil
1 teaspoon lime juice
15 g (½ oz) fresh coriander
(cilantro) leaves, plus extra
to serve
2 teaspoons tamarind paste
1 teaspoon soft brown sugar

As a carb lover, there is nothing I enjoy
more than a filling pasta, rice or noodle dish.
From Asian-inspired to traditional Italian
fare, there is something in this chapter you
are bound to love. Not only are these meals
quick and easy to cook, they are also packed
with flavour – you'd never even know they're
low FODMAP.

Pasta, Rice and Noodles,

Oh My!

This authentic carbonara is lightened up by the addition of zoodles. The zucchini (courgette) not only adds more fibre to the meal, but it has a mild enough flavour that it doesn't detract from that much-loved creamy, bacony taste. You can omit the zoodles, if you like – I get that they're not for everyone! Just replace with 50 g (1¾ oz) uncooked pasta. I also use bacon instead of the more traditional speck or pancetta, simply because it's is easier to come by. Feel free to substitute the bacon for a more traditional option, as it's delicious either way. If you don't have a spiraliser, you can make the zoodles by simply cutting the zucchini into thin strips with a knife.

Cream-free carbonara with zoodles

Prep time: 5 minutes
Cook time: 20 minutes
Serves: 2

150 g (5½ oz) spaghetti or
   pasta of your choice
2 eggs
¾ cup (80 g) grated parmesan,
   plus extra to serve
½ tablespoon garlic-infused
   olive oil
200 g (7 oz) bacon, diced
200 g (7 oz) zoodles (approx.
   1 zucchini/courgette)
½ teaspoon black pepper

Cook the pasta in a saucepan of salted water according to the packet instructions, but do not drain.

Meanwhile, place the eggs and parmesan in a bowl and whisk to combine.

While the pasta is cooking, heat the garlic oil in a frying pan over medium–high heat and fry the bacon until brown and caramelised. Turn off the heat.

Once the pasta is cooked, use tongs to take it out of the pan and add it straight to the pan with the bacon. Quickly add the egg and parmesan mixture and stir with the tongs until the cheese is melted. Add some pasta water, a little at a time, until a nice sauce develops.

Place the zoodles in a microwave-safe bowl with 2 tablespoons water. Microwave for 1–2 minutes on high until cooked to your liking.

Drain the zoodles of excess water and add to the pan with the pasta and bacon. Toss together, season with pepper and a little extra grated parmesan, then serve.

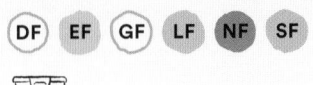

(DF) (EF) (GF) (LF) **NF** (SF)

This dish is made in one pot and comes together in about 20 minutes, making it perfect for a quick weeknight dinner. It's creamy, full of flavour and is sure to become a firm family favourite.

Creamy Tuscan chicken penne

Prep time: 5 minutes
Cook time: 20 minutes
Serves: 4

200 g (7 oz) penne or pasta
  of your choice (see Tips)
2 tablespoons garlic-infused
  olive oil
250 g (9 oz) skinless chicken
  breasts, diced
100 g (3½ oz) cherry tomatoes,
  left whole, or regular tomatoes,
  roughly chopped
1¼ cups (55 g) baby spinach
1 teaspoon dried basil
1 teaspoon dried oregano
1 teaspoon dried chives
1½ teaspoons salt
¼ teaspoon black pepper
600 ml (21 fl oz) lactose-free milk
  (see Tips)
2½ tablespoons cornflour
  (cornstarch) mixed with ¼ cup
  (60 ml) cold water (see Tip,
  page 20)
20 g (¾ oz) grated parmesan

Bring a saucepan of salted water to the boil and cook the pasta for a few minutes less than what the packet instructions suggest. You want it to be a little more al dente than usual. Drain and set aside.

Heat the garlic oil in a saucepan over medium heat and cook the chicken until browned, about 3–4 minutes.

Add the tomato, spinach, dried herbs and salt and pepper, and sauté until the tomato has softened and the spinach has wilted.

Add the milk and bring to the boil, then add the cornflour slurry and reduce the heat to a simmer. The sauce should be nice and thick.

Mix in the parmesan, remove from the heat and allow the sauce to cool slightly before adding the cooked pasta.

Serve straight away or store in the fridge for 3–4 days or in portions in the freezer for up to 3 months.

For the best results, allow to thaw overnight in the fridge, then heat in the microwave for 2–3 minutes, stirring halfway through, until evenly heated. You can also reheat it from frozen in the microwave for 4–6 minutes.

Tips: If using gluten-free pasta, you'll still need to make sure the sauce has cooled slightly before adding it, as it can easily overcook the pasta.

This recipe works best with lactose-free or regular milk. You can substitute it for a dairy-free alternative, but this may change the flavour profile and texture of the dish. If the finished sauce is thinner than you'd like, add a little more cornflour slurry to thicken it.

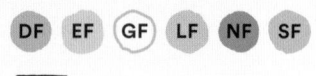

If you have never had puttanesca before, then you should definitely make this. It is so flavoursome and hits the perfect balance of sweet, salty and tangy – truly lip-smackingly good! This sauce is also very versatile and can be served with rice or any grain of your choice instead of the pasta.

Chicken puttanesca pasta

Prep time: 5 minutes
Cook time: 50 minutes
Serves: 4

1½ tablespoons garlic-infused olive oil
800 g (1 lb 12 oz) boneless, skinless chicken thighs, cut into 2–3 cm (¾–1¼ in) dice
1 × 400 g (14 oz) tin tomatoes
50 g (1¾ oz) pitted kalamata (black) olives, halved
¼ cup (45 g) capers, drained and rinsed
1 teaspoon chilli flakes
1 teaspoon dried chives
1 teaspoon dried basil
1 teaspoon dried oregano
1 teaspoon dried parsley
¼ teaspoon ground cinnamon
1 teaspoon salt
1 tablespoon cornflour (cornstarch) mixed with 2 tablespoons cold water (see Tip, page 20)
250 g (9 oz) pasta of your choice

Heat the garlic oil in a stockpot over medium–high heat and fry the chicken for 3–4 minutes until browned. Add all the remaining ingredients, except the cornflour slurry and pasta, with 200 ml (7 fl oz) water and bring to the boil. Once boiling, reduce the heat to medium–low and simmer for 30–45 minutes until the chicken is cooked through.

Add the cornflour slurry and stir to thicken the sauce.

Cook the pasta according to the packet instructions, then drain. Combine with the sauce and enjoy straight away or store in the fridge for 3–4 days, or in portions in the freezer for up to 3 months.

For the best results, allow to thaw overnight in the fridge, then heat in the microwave for 2–3 minutes, stirring halfway through, until evenly heated. You can also reheat it from frozen in the microwave for 4–6 minutes.

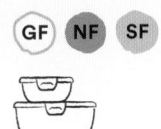

GF NF SF

Pasta bakes make dinnertime a breeze. No waiting for water to boil or sauce to cook – just place everything in one dish, pop it in the oven and walk away. I created this particular recipe on a day when I wanted something comforting but full of veggies and flavour. I also didn't want to stand around in the kitchen, so I threw it in the oven and hoped for the best. Luckily, it turned out to be one of the simplest, nicest meals, and I now eat it on repeat. Thank me later.

Veggie and olive pasta bake

Prep time: 5 minutes
Cook time: 30 minutes
Serves: 4

200 g (7 oz) pasta of your choice
250 g (9 oz) carrot, sliced into half-moons approx. 5 mm (¼ in) thick
175 g (6 oz) red capsicum (pepper), cut into 5 mm (¼ in) thick slices
200 g (7 oz) zucchini (courgette), sliced into half-moons approx. 5 mm (¼ in) thick
50 g (1¾ oz) pitted kalamata (black) olives, sliced
1 tablespoon dried chives
1 teaspoon sweet paprika
1½ teaspoons dried parsley
2 teaspoons dried oregano
1½ teaspoons dried basil
2 teaspoons salt
1 teaspoon black pepper
1 × 400 g (14 oz) tin tomatoes
2 low-FODMAP chicken stock cubes
50 ml (1¾ fl oz) garlic-infused olive oil
¼ cup (35 g) feta cheese (optional)

Preheat the oven to 200°C (400°F).

Add all the ingredients, except the feta cheese, to a deep baking dish or tray with 1 cup (250 ml) water. Mix well and cover will aluminium foil.

Bake for 30 minutes or until the pasta is cooked through. Crumble the feta cheese on top (if using) and enjoy straight away or store in the fridge for 3–4 days, or in portions in the freezer for up to 3 months.

For the best results, allow to thaw overnight in the fridge, then heat in the microwave for 2–3 minutes, stirring halfway through, until evenly heated. You can also reheat it from frozen in the microwave for 4–6 minutes.

Tips: This also works really well as a side dish to the Pesto-stuffed chicken with balsamic reduction (page 65).

Feel free to add chicken, firm tofu, ¼ cup (40 g) tinned chickpeas or any other protein if you want to bulk this dish out even further.

A word of advice: you're probably going to want to double or triple this recipe and keep it in the fridge or freezer for those days when only pasta will do. It is so damn good, you'll want to eat it all the time! I have allowed for extra sauce so you can make the dish as 'saucy' as you desire. Any leftover sauce can be stored in the fridge for up to 2 weeks and used for pizza sauce, another pasta dish or even as a dipping sauce for something like the Baked arancini on page 130.

Spinach and ricotta cannelloni

Prep time: 20 minutes
Cook time: 20 minutes
Serves: 4

8 fresh or dried lasagne sheets

Filling
2⅓ cups (120 g) baby spinach
    or 3 blocks (75 g/2¾ oz each)
    frozen spinach
1½ cups (375 g) ricotta cheese
    or lactose-free alternative
    (see Tips)
2 eggs, lightly beaten
½ teaspoon dried chives
½ teaspoon dried basil
¼ teaspoon dried oregano
⅛ teaspoon nutmeg
½ teaspoon black pepper
½ teaspoon salt
35 g (1¼ oz) grated parmesan
120 g (4½ oz) grated mozzarella
    cheese, plus extra for topping
2 tablespoons garlic-infused
    olive oil

Sauce
1 quantity Napoli sauce
    (page 214; see Tips)

Preheat the oven to 180°C (350°F).

Cook the lasagne sheets according to the packet instructions, then set aside.

If you are using fresh spinach, blanch it by putting it in a saucepan of boiling water for 1–2 minutes or until wilted.

Mix all the filling ingredients together in a bowl.

In a deep baking dish or tray, place a couple of large spoonfuls of the sauce and spread it out evenly over the base. It doesn't need to be a lot – just enough to prevent the pasta from sticking.

Grab a lasagne sheet and spread 2 tablespoons of the filling all over the sheet. Gently roll it up and place it, seam side down, in the dish. Repeat with the remaining lasagne sheets and filling. Once all the cannelloni are rolled, top with enough sauce to generously cover the pasta. Sprinkle the extra mozzarella on top and bake for 15–20 minutes or until the cheese is melted and golden brown.

The cannelloni can be stored in the fridge for 3–4 days or in portions in the freezer for up to 3 months.

For the best results, allow to thaw overnight in the fridge, then heat in the microwave for 2–3 minutes, stirring halfway through, until evenly heated. You can also reheat it from frozen in the microwave for 4–6 minutes (see Tips).

Tips: While the amount of ricotta used here is low FODMAP, if you are lactose intolerant you can easily substitute it for lactose-free ricotta.

Depending on how saucy you like your cannelloni, you may not need all the Napoli sauce. If you have some left over and are reheating the cannelloni, add some extra sauce before or after reheating, as it can become a little dry.

Risotto is such a comforting dish – warm, creamy and oh so filling! This recipe has been my go-to for risotto for years, as it's simple to cook and full of flavour. I also love that the pumpkin (squash) gives it a nice golden hue. The trick to any good risotto is to cook it until the rice is al dente, keep it a little wet and serve immediately. This is because the rice will continue to absorb the liquid as it cools, reaching the perfect consistency on the plate.

Creamy pumpkin and pine nut risotto

Prep time: 5 minutes
Cook time: 30 minutes
Serves: 4

5 cups (1.25 litres) water or
  Low-FODMAP chicken stock
  (page 217)
2 low-FODMAP chicken stock
  cubes (omit if using chicken
  stock)
1½ tablespoons garlic-infused
  olive oil
320 g (11¼ oz) kabocha
  (Japanese) pumpkin (squash),
  skin removed,
  cut into 5 cm (2 in) dice
1 cup (220 g) arborio rice
1 teaspoon salt
1 teaspoon black pepper
1 teaspoon dried thyme
½ teaspoon dried rosemary
1 tablespoon dried chives
¼ teaspoon ground turmeric
100 g (3½ oz) zucchini
  (courgette), cut into 1–2 cm
  (¼–¾ in) dice
25 g (1 oz) grated parmesan
20 g (¾ oz) toasted pine nuts,
  to garnish

Bring the water and stock cubes (or chicken stock) to the boil in a large saucepan. Once boiling, reduce the heat to a low simmer.

In another saucepan, heat the garlic oil over medium–high heat and add half the pumpkin, the rice, salt, pepper, herbs and spices and toast for 2–3 minutes.

Carefully add one to two ladles of warm stock to the pan with the rice and stir until most of the liquid has been absorbed. Add the zucchini, then continue to add stock, one ladle at a time, until the rice is half cooked, about 10 minutes. Add the remaining pumpkin.

Continue adding more stock, cooking in between each addition, until the rice is al dente. The constant stirring and slow addition of the hot stock will release the starches from the rice, making the dish nice and creamy.

Once the rice is al dente, remove the pan from the heat and stir in the parmesan. Garnish with pine nuts, serve and enjoy.

Tip: Leftovers can be used to make Baked arancini (page 130).

Vegetarian lasagne is a great hearty and flavoursome meal option, and since there is no meat sauce or béchamel in this version, it comes together quite quickly. The roasted vegetables give this lasagne a lovely umami-rich flavour that will satisfy even the most devoted meat-lovers.

Easy vegetarian lasagne

Prep time: 5 minutes
Cook time: 35 minutes
Serves: 6–8

8 fresh or dried lasagne sheets
1 large eggplant (aubergine),
    cut into 1 cm (½in) thick strips
2 medium zucchini (courgettes),
    cut into 1 cm (½ in) thick strips
2 tablespoons extra-virgin
    olive oil
250 g (9 oz) fresh ricotta cheese
    (see Tips, page 40)
1 egg
¼ teaspoon each salt and
    black pepper, plus extra for
    seasoning
1 tablespoon grated parmesan
100 g (3½ oz) grated mozzarella
    cheese
350 g (12 oz) Napoli sauce
    (page 214)

Preheat the oven to 180°C (350°F).

Cook the lasagne sheets according to the packet instructions.

Put the eggplant and zucchini on baking trays, drizzle with the oil and season with extra salt and pepper. Roast for 10 minutes, until the vegetables are tender. Alternatively, cook the vegetables on a chargrill pan until tender.

Meanwhile, combine the ricotta, egg, salt, pepper, parmesan and ¼ cup (35 g) of the mozzarella in a bowl and mix to combine.

Spread 2 tablespoons of the Napoli sauce in the base of a deep baking dish and top with a layer of lasagne sheets, followed by a layer of roasted eggplant. Top with 2–3 tablespoons of the ricotta mix and spread evenly over the roasted eggplant, then spread 3–4 tablespoons of Napoli sauce over the ricotta mix. Place another layer of lasagne sheets on top and repeat this process with the roasted zucchini. Finish with the remaining lasagne sheets and another 4 tablespoons sauce and the remaining ricotta mix. Top with the remaining mozzarella and bake for 20–25 minutes or until the cheese is golden and brown.

Enjoy straight away or store in the fridge for 3–4 days or in portions in the freezer for up to 3 months.

For the best results, allow to thaw overnight in the fridge, then heat in the microwave for 2–3 minutes, stirring halfway through, until evenly heated. You can also reheat it from frozen in the microwave for 4–6 minutes.

Tip: I like the Mediterranean flavours of the eggplant and zucchini, but you could use ¼ of a roasted kabocha (Japanese) pumpkin (squash) or 2–3 capsicums (peppers) instead.

The beauty of this dish is not only that it is made in one pan or that it comes together in 25 minutes but that there is also no need to pre-boil the gnocchi. Did you know that gnocchi can be cooked directly in the pan with the sauce?! Day. Made.

Creamy pesto salmon gnocchi

Prep time: 5 minutes
Cook time: 20 minutes
Serves: 4

2 tablespoons extra-virgin
   olive oil
300 g (10½ oz) salmon fillet,
   skin removed (see Tips)
1½ tablespoons plain
   (all-purpose) flour of
   your choice or cornflour
   (cornstarch)
1 cup (250 ml) water or
   Low-FODMAP chicken stock
   (page 217)
1 low-FODMAP chicken stock
   cube (omit if using chicken
   stock)
1 cup (250 ml) lactose-free milk
   or milk of your choice
   (see Tips)
500 g (1 lb 2 oz) potato gnocchi
2½ cups (150 g) broccoli florets,
   quartered
2 tablespoons Basil pesto
   (page 206; see Tips) or
   store-bought pesto if tolerated
1¾ cups (80 g) baby spinach
grated parmesan, to serve
   (optional)
salt and black pepper, to taste

Heat half the oil in a frying pan over high heat, then reduce the heat to medium and add the salmon fillet. Season with salt and pepper and cook for 4–5 minutes on each side (lower the heat if it browns too quickly) until just cooked through. Remove from the pan and set aside.

Add the remaining oil and return the pan to high heat. Add the flour and whisk for 1–2 minutes, then slowly add the water and stock cube (or chicken stock) and milk. Bring to the boil, whisking continuously so that it doesn't stick to the bottom of the pan. The liquid should begin to thicken.

Reduce the heat to a simmer and add the gnocchi and broccoli florets. Add the pesto and cook for 2–3 minutes until the gnocchi is soft and the broccoli is cooked, then turn off the heat and add the spinach. Stir through until the spinach has wilted. Finally, flake in the cooked salmon and season with salt and pepper if needed. Top with some parmesan, if you like.

Tips: You can substitute the salmon for chicken breast, if you prefer.

If you're making your own pesto, freeze some in 1 tablespoon portions for up to 3 months, and simply throw in with the milk and stock, or leave to defrost first in the fridge overnight.

This recipe calls for lactose-free milk, but you can use regular milk if tolerated. Dairy-free milk can be used as well, though it will alter the flavour of the dish.

This is a very nostalgic meal for me, as it reminds me of my grandmother. She used to make it regularly, and I have fond memories of eating it with her and my sister. The lemon cuts through the richness of the dish and gives a lovely, subtle tang that's complemented by the salty feta cheese. It also makes a great side dish served with a meat of your choice.

Spanakorizo
Greek spinach rice

Prep time: 20–25 minutes
Cook time: 25 minutes
Serves: 4

120 g (4¼ oz) long-grain
white rice, rinsed and drained
2 tablespoons extra-virgin
olive oil
2 tablespoons garlic-infused
olive oil
60 g (2 oz) spring onion
(scallion), green part only
1 tablespoon finely chopped dill
1 tablespoon finely chopped
parsley
400 g (14 oz) baby spinach
(see Tips)
4 cups (1 litre) water or
Low-FODMAP chicken stock
(page 217; see Tips)
2 low-FODMAP chicken stock
cubes (omit if using chicken
stock)
2 cups (500 ml) tomato passata
(puréed tomatoes)
1 tablespoon lemon juice
¼ cup (35 g) feta cheese,
crumbled (optional)
salt and black pepper, to taste

Wash the rice three or four times until the water runs clear, then soak the rice in cold water for 10–15 minutes.

While the rice is soaking, heat the oils in a large frying pan over medium–high heat and fry the spring onion, dill and parsley for 1–2 minutes. Add the spinach in batches, waiting until each batch is wilted before adding more.

Drain the rice and add it to the pan with the herbs and the spinach. Add the water and stock cubes (or chicken stock) and the passata. Bring to the boil, then reduce the heat to a rapid simmer and cook for 20 minutes, or until the rice is al dente (the rice will continue to cook in the residual heat, so don't overcook it at this point). Rest in the pan for 5–10 minutes. Season with salt and pepper to taste, add the lemon juice and mix through. Scatter the feta cheese on top (if using) and serve.

Tips: If you prefer less spinach, you can reduce the quantity to 300 g (10½ oz) – make sure to reduce the quantity of water (or stock) to 800 ml (28 fl oz) too.

You can also reduce the amount of liquid if you simply prefer your spanakorizo less soupy – anywhere between 800 ml (28 fl oz) and 1 litre (35 fl oz/4 cups) will work.

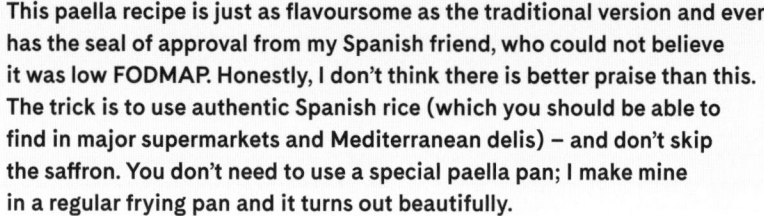

This paella recipe is just as flavoursome as the traditional version and even has the seal of approval from my Spanish friend, who could not believe it was low FODMAP. Honestly, I don't think there is better praise than this. The trick is to use authentic Spanish rice (which you should be able to find in major supermarkets and Mediterranean delis) – and don't skip the saffron. You don't need to use a special paella pan; I make mine in a regular frying pan and it turns out beautifully.

Prawn and calamari paella

Prep time: 5 minutes
Cook time: 50 minutes
Serves: 4–6

¼ cup (60 ml) extra-virgin olive oil
2 tablespoons garlic-infused olive oil
120 g (4¼ oz/approx. ½ large) red capsicum (pepper), finely diced
350 g (12 oz/approx. 3 small) tomatoes, finely diced
30 g (1 oz) spring onion (scallion) tops, green part only
pinch of saffron threads
1 bay leaf
1 teaspoon sweet paprika
½ teaspoon smoked paprika
200 g (7 oz) calamari, cut into bite-sized pieces or rings
2 cups (440 g) Spanish rice or medium-grain white rice, rinsed and drained
30 g (1 oz) fresh flat-leaf (Italian) parsley
4 cups (1 litre) Low-FODMAP chicken stock (page 217)
400 g (14 oz) prawns (shrimp), shells on
80 g (2¾ oz) green beans, cut into small pieces about the size of peas
salt and black pepper, to taste
lemon wedges, to serve

Heat the oils in a large frying pan (or paella pan if you have one) over high heat. Add the diced capsicum, tomato, spring onion and spices and cook over medium–high heat for 10–15 minutes. Season with salt and pepper.

Next, add the calamari and cook for a couple of minutes before adding the rice and half the parsley. Cook the rice for 1–2 minutes, then add the chicken stock and bring to the boil. Reduce the heat to medium–high and cook for 15–20 minutes. It should be more than a simmer; you need the rice to cook and absorb most of the liquid. From this point on, it is important not to stir the rice but rather just shake the pan. You want the rice to form a crust known as socarrat, meaning 'to scorch'.

After 10–15 minutes, add the prawns and cook for 5–10 minutes before adding the green beans on top. Cook for another 5 minutes until most of the liquid has been absorbed and the prawns are cooked through.

Remove the pan from the heat and cover with aluminium foil, then drape a tea towel (dish towel) on top or cover with a lid. Leave to sit for 10 minutes. After 10 minutes, sprinkle the remaining parsley on top and serve with lemon wedges.

DF **EF** **GF** **LF** **NF**

This is a delicious and easy-to-make dish that brings the essence of Japanese street food right to your kitchen. This recipe features tender chicken pieces stir-fried with crisp vegetables and savoury noodles all tossed in a mouthwatering, tangy-sweet sauce. Perfect for busy weeknights or when you're craving something different.

Chicken yakisoba-style noodles

Prep time: 10 minutes
Cook time: 20 minutes
Serves: 2

150 g (5½ oz) rice noodles or
    egg noodles if tolerated
2 tablespoons garlic-infused
    olive oil, plus extra if needed
380 g (13½ oz) skinless chicken
    breasts, cut into 1 cm (½ in)
    slices
120 g (4¼ oz) red capsicum
    (pepper), cut into 5 mm–1 cm
    (¼–½ in) strips
80 g (2¾ oz) carrot, cut into
    3 mm–1 cm (⅛ in) strips
100 g (3½ oz) common or white
    cabbage, cut into 5 mm–1 cm
    (¼–½ in) strips
20 g (¾ oz) spring onion
    (scallion), green part only
salt and black pepper

Sauce
¼ cup (60 ml) gluten-free
    Worcestershire sauce
1½ tablespoons soy sauce
1½ tablespoons tomato sauce
    (ketchup)
1 tablespoon oyster sauce
1½ teaspoons soft brown sugar
1 teaspoon garlic-infused olive oil

Cook the noodles according to the packet instructions, then drain and rinse under cold water. Set aside.

Combine all the sauce ingredients in a bowl and mix well.

Heat the garlic oil in a large frying pan or wok over medium–high heat and fry the chicken with some salt and pepper for 3–4 minutes until browned. Remove from the pan and set aside.

Add all the vegetables, except the spring onion tops, to the pan and fry over medium–high heat for 5–10 minutes until softened. Add some extra oil if needed.

Add the sauce, chicken, noodles and spring onion tops. Stir through until the noodles are warm and the sauce has thickened. Serve and enjoy.

Ideal for a quick weeknight dinner or a special meal, this pad see ew captures the essence of Thai street food: tender beef, chewy noodles and a rich, sweet-and-salty sauce. The bicarbonate of soda (baking soda) helps to keep the meat tender and really is a game changer for beef stir-fries in general.

Beef pad see ew

Prep time: 10 minutes, plus marinating
Cook time: 20 minutes
Serves: 4

1 tablespoon soy sauce
1 teaspoon bicarbonate of soda (baking soda)
260 g (9¼ oz) sirloin, flank or skirt steak, cut into 2 mm (¹⁄₁₆ in) thick slices
400 g (14 oz) fresh or 200 g (7 oz) dried thick rice noodles (see Tip)
2 tablespoons garlic-infused olive oil
150 g (5½ oz) Chinese broccoli (gai lan) or broccolini, stems cut into 2 cm (¾ in) lengths on the diagonal
1 egg

Sauce
100 ml (3½ fl oz) soy sauce
¼ cup (60 ml) oyster sauce
1 tablespoon white vinegar
1 tablespoon soft brown sugar

Combine the soy sauce and bicarb soda in a bowl. Add the steak, mix and leave to marinate in the fridge for 1–2 hours.

Cook the rice noodles according to the packet instructions (if using dried). Drain and rinse under cold water.

While the noodles are cooking, make the sauce by mixing all the ingredients in a bowl.

Add half the sauce to the cooled noodles and mix to coat.

In a large frying pan or wok, heat 1 tablespoon of the garlic oil over medium–high heat and fry the beef slices for 1 minute on each side. Don't move them around too much in the pan; you want to get a nice char on them. Fry until the meat is almost cooked through, then remove from the pan.

Add the remaining oil to the pan and cook the broccoli for 4–5 minutes until it begins to soften, then push it to one side and crack in the egg. Scramble the egg and mix it with the broccolini, then remove from the pan.

Add the rice noodles to the pan, but don't stir immediately. Allow the noodles to sit in the hot pan for 1 minute to get a bit of colour on them, then return the beef, broccolini, egg and remaining sauce to the pan. Toss briefly to combine, then serve.

Tip: Fresh rice noodles will elevate this dish to a truly authentic experience, so I recommend using them, rather than dried noodles, if you can find them (they're usually available at Asian grocery stores).

Bright. Colourful. Healthy. Yet, the hero of this dish is definitely the dressing: a little sweet, a little salty and so unique. Here, simple ingredients come together to create a delicious meal that is perfect for lunch or dinner.

Sesame chicken noodle bowl

Prep time: 10 minutes
Cook time: 20 minutes
Serves: 4

2 tablespoons extra-virgin
   olive oil
500 g (1 lb 2 oz) skinless chicken
   breasts, cut into 2–3 cm
   (¾–1¼ in) dice
2 tablespoons soy sauce
3⅓ cups (200 g) broccoli florets
220 g (7¾ oz) thick rice noodles
200 g (7 oz) carrot, grated
160 g (5¾ oz) frozen edamame,
   thawed
1 tablespoon sesame seeds,
   to garnish
salt and black pepper

Tahini dressing
80 g (2¾ oz) tahini
50 ml (1¾ fl oz) soy sauce
15 ml (½ fl oz) sesame oil
15 ml (½ fl oz) rice-wine vinegar
15 ml (½ fl oz) garlic-infused
   olive oil
1½ teaspoons soft brown sugar

Combine all the dressing ingredients in a bowl with 65 ml (2¼ fl oz) water and whisk until combined.

Heat the oil in a frying pan over medium heat and add the diced chicken, soy sauce and some salt and pepper. Fry for 10 minutes until the chicken is browned and no longer pink.

Bring a saucepan of water to the boil and cook the broccoli for 5 minutes, or until cooked to your liking, then drain and set aside.

Cook the noodles according to the packet instructions, then drain and rinse under cold water. Place the noodles in a bowl, add half the dressing and toss to combine.

To serve, divide the noodles, chicken, broccoli, carrot and edamame between four serving bowls. Drizzle some of the reserved tahini dressing on top and sprinkle with sesame seeds.

Chicken is arguably the most popular meat in the Western world. It's relatively cheap, high in protein and can be used in so many dishes without taking on the main flavour profile. It is such a staple in my cooking that it was difficult to narrow it down to just the recipes in this chapter. I've tried to showcase just how much variety there is when cooking low FODMAP – with classic meals from chicken pot pie to Middle Eastern sharwarma-style chicken, there doesn't need to be a shortage of options in your LoFo kitchen.

Chicken Dinner

= Winner

I love a good bowl. It's a very close cousin to the salad but with a little more substance and satisfying presentation – after all, we do eat with our eyes. These Vietnamese-style bowls are simple to make and are really all about the chicken and the dressing. I use nuoc mam sauce as the dressing, which is primarily used as a dipping sauce, but it works so well with these flavours and elevates the beautifully sweet-and-salty chicken.

Vietnamese-style chicken bowl with nuoc mam

Prep time: 5 minutes, plus marinating
Cook time: 25 minutes
Serves: 4

400 g (14 oz) boneless, skinless chicken thighs
200 g (7 oz) rice noodles
1–2 tablespoons extra-virgin olive oil
200 g (7 oz) mixed leaves
100 g (3½ oz) thinly sliced carrot
2 radishes, thinly sliced
handful of fresh coriander (cilantro) leaves
160 g (5¾ oz) cucumber, thinly sliced
20 g (¾ oz) spring onion (scallion), green part only, thinly sliced
lime wedges, to serve (optional)

Chicken marinade
1 tablespoon soy sauce
1 tablespoon fish sauce
25 g (1 oz) soft brown sugar
3 teaspoons lime juice
1 teaspoon garlic-infused olive oil
1 teaspoon minced or crushed ginger

Nuoc mam
35 g (1¼ oz) caster (superfine) sugar
2½ tablespoons lime juice
2 tablespoons fish sauce
1 teaspoon garlic-infused olive oil
1 teaspoon diced fresh red chilli

Combine all the marinade ingredients in a large bowl. Add the chicken thighs and mix well. Cover the bowl with plastic wrap and marinate in the fridge for 2–4 hours or overnight (the longer the better).

For the nuoc mam, combine ½ cup (125 ml) water and the caster sugar in a saucepan and heat over medium heat until the sugar dissolves. Leave to cool completely, then add the remaining ingredients and mix well.

Cook the rice noodles according to the packet instructions, then drain and rinse under cold water.

Heat the oil in a frying pan over medium–high heat and cook the chicken for 10–15 minutes until it is lightly charred on the outside and no longer pink, then slice.

Divide the noodles, chicken and salad ingredients between four serving bowls. Top with the nuoc mam and the lime wedges, if desired, and enjoy either warmed up or cold from the fridge.

Tip: Feel free to substitute any of the ingredients, such as using rice instead of rice noodles. Create and adjust as you see fit.

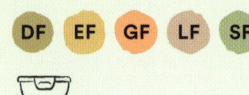

Combining spiced chicken and rice with sweet cranberries and crunchy almonds, this dish is the flavour sensation you didn't know you needed! It is very easy to prepare and comes together in the one roasting tin. Perfect for a cosy weeknight dinner or a special gathering, this recipe is a crowd-pleaser that strikes the perfect balance between savoury, sweet and crunchy. Get ready to add a new favourite to your dinner rotation.

Shawarma-style chicken with spiced rice

Prep time: 5 minutes, plus marinating
Cook time: 45 minutes
Serves: 6

6 skinless, boneless chicken thighs (about 900 g/2 lb)
1 tablespoon extra-virgin olive oil
¼ cup (25 g) toasted flaked almonds, to garnish
fresh flat-leaf (Italian) parsley, to garnish

Spice rub
1½ teaspoons ground coriander
1½ teaspoons ground cumin
1 teaspoon ground cardamon
1 teaspoon smoked paprika
½ teaspoon salt
¼ teaspoon black pepper
¼ teaspoon cayenne pepper
¼ cup (60 ml) lemon juice
1 tablespoon garlic-infused olive oil

Rice
½ tablespoon garlic-infused olive oil
300 g (10½ oz) medium-grain white rice, rinsed and drained
2 low-FODMAP chicken stock cubes
1 teaspoon salt
¼ teaspoon black pepper
1 teaspoon ground cardamon
¼ teaspoon ground cinnamon
30 g (1 oz) dried cranberries
½ tablespoon dried chives

Combine the spice rub ingredients, except the garlic oil, in a large bowl, add the chicken thighs and marinate in the fridge for 1–2 hours.

Heat the oil in a frying pan or chargrill pan over medium–high heat and sear the chicken for 1–2 minutes on each side until browned, then remove from the pan and set aside.

Preheat the oven to 180°C (350°F).

To a large, deep roasting tin, add all the rice ingredients along with 3½ cups (875 ml) water. Stir to make sure everything is well combined, then cover with aluminium foil and bake for 20 minutes.

Add the chicken to the rice and bake uncovered for 10–15 minutes until the rice is cooked and the chicken is no longer pink.

Top with the flaked almonds and fresh parsley to serve. Enjoy straight away or store in the fridge for 3–4 days, or in portions in the freezer for up to 3 months.

For the best results, allow to thaw overnight in the fridge, then heat in the microwave for 2–3 minutes, stirring halfway through, until evenly heated. You can also reheat it from frozen in the microwave for 4–6 minutes.

One thing that really makes a salad is a little crunch! The addition of nuts or seeds adds another textural dimension that can really elevate a simple salad. The maple seed and nut clusters in this recipe not only add some sweetness and excitement but extra healthy fats, too.

Roasted pumpkin, chicken and goat's cheese salad with maple clusters

Prep time: 5 minutes
Cook time: 50 minutes
Serves: 4

¼ cup (60 ml) pure maple syrup
¼ cup (40 g) pepitas (pumpkin
   seeds)
¼ cup (30 g) walnuts
250 g (9 oz) kabocha (Japanese)
   pumpkin (squash), skin
   removed, cut into 3 cm
   (1¼ in) dice
⅓ cup (80 ml) extra-virgin
   olive oil
400 g (14 oz) skinless, boneless
   chicken thighs
4 cups (200 g) baby spinach
200 g (7 oz) rocket (arugula)
¾ cup (130 g) pomegranate
   seeds
100 g (3½ oz) goat's cheese
salt and black pepper

Dressing
½ cup (125 ml) extra-virgin
   olive oil
2 tablespoons white vinegar
½ teaspoon salt
¼ teaspoon black pepper
¼ teaspoon ground cumin

Preheat the oven to 180°C (350°F).

Add the maple syrup, pepitas and walnuts to a frying pan and cook over medium–high heat for 3–4 minutes until the maple syrup begins to bubble. Continue cooking for a further 2–3 minutes, stirring constantly, then transfer to a plate lined with baking paper. Allow to cool.

Place the pumpkin in a roasting tin, drizzle 2 tablespoons of the oil on top and season with salt and pepper. Roast for 20–25 minutes or until the pumpkin is soft and cooked through.

Make the dressing by combining all the ingredients in a bowl.

Heat the remaining oil in a frying pan over high heat. Add the chicken thighs, season with salt and pepper, and turn to brown. Once the chicken is well browned, reduce the heat to medium and continue cooking until the chicken is cooked through and no longer pink, about 15–20 minutes. Allow the chicken to cool slightly, then shred with a fork.

In a salad bowl, combine the spinach, rocket, shredded chicken, roasted pumpkin, pomegranate seeds and goat's cheese. Finally, break up the maple clusters (they should have formed a solid piece) with your hands and add to the salad. Add the dressing and toss to coat evenly.

Tip: The maple nut clusters are also great as a snack, or on top of yoghurt.

 DF EF GF LF SF

Be dinner-guest ready in a flash with this pesto-stuffed chicken. This dish may sound fancy, but you will be surprised how easy it is to make. All it takes is blitzing up some pesto (page 206), cooking some chicken and reducing some balsamic vinegar. Scout's honour!

Pesto-stuffed chicken with balsamic reduction

Prep time: 10 minutes
Cook time: 25 minutes
Serves: 4

4 skinless chicken breasts
4 tablespoons Basil pesto or Kale pesto (page 206)
2 tablespoons extra-virgin olive oil

Balsamic glaze
½ cup (60 ml) balsamic vinegar
1 tablespoon soft brown sugar

Preheat the oven to 180°C (350°F).

Using a sharp knife, cut a pocket into the thickest part of each chicken breast. Using a teaspoon, fill the cavities with 1 tablespoon pesto each.

Heat the oil in an ovenproof frying pan over medium–high heat and cook the stuffed chicken breasts for 2–4 minutes on each side until golden brown. Transfer to a baking tray lined with baking paper. Bake for 15–20 minutes, depending on the thickness of the chicken, until cooked through and no longer pink (the juices should run clear when the thickest part of the chicken is pierced with a knife).

While the chicken is cooking, combine the vinegar and sugar in a small saucepan and bring to the boil over high heat, then reduce the heat to low and simmer for 10 minutes until the glaze has thickened.

Drizzle the glaze over the chicken and serve with salad, vegetables, or a pasta or grain of your choice.

Bowls are such an easy win for a weeknight dinner, and this is one of my favourites: perfectly seasoned chicken, tangy fragrant lime rice and a creamy sauce that ties it all together.

Chicken burrito bowl with coriander lime rice and creamy spiced mayo

Prep time: 10 minutes, plus marinating
Cook time: 45 minutes
Serves: 4

Chicken
600 g (1 lb 5 oz) skinless chicken breast, cut into 2 cm (¾ in) cubes
2 tablespoons extra-virgin olive oil, plus 1–2 tablespoons extra for cooking the chicken
2 teaspoons ground coriander
1 tablespoon ground cumin
2 teaspoons sweet paprika
1 tablespoon lime juice
1 tablespoon garlic-infused olive oil
1 tablespoon oregano
1 teaspoon salt
1 teaspoon chilli flakes or powder, or to taste

Lime rice
1 cup (200 g) long-grain white rice, rinsed and drained
2 cups (500 ml) water or Low-FODMAP chicken stock (page 217)
2 low-FODMAP chicken stock cubes (omit if using chicken stock)
juice of ½ lime
20 g (¾ oz) fresh coriander (cilantro), finely chopped

For the chicken, combine all the ingredients in a bowl and marinate in the fridge for 2 hours or overnight.

To make the lime rice, add the rice to a large saucepan with the water and stock cubes (or chicken stock). Bring to the boil over high heat, then reduce the heat to low, cover and simmer for 15–20 minutes until the rice is cooked through. Add the lime juice and fresh coriander and gently mix through.

While the rice is cooking, heat 1–2 tablespoons of extra-virgin olive oil in a frying pan over medium–high heat and cook the marinated chicken for 10–15 minutes, or until cooked through and nicely charred on the edges.

For the spiced chickpeas, add all the ingredients to a frying pan and cook over medium–high heat for 10 minutes, or until the chickpeas are cooked to your liking.

Mix all the spiced mayo sauce ingredients in a small bowl.

Serve the chicken over the lime rice with some chickpeas, diced tomato, avocado and corn. Serve the spiced mayo sauce on the side, along with lime wedges, if desired.

Spiced chickpeas

1 cup (165 g) tinned chickpeas, drained and rinsed
1 tablespoon extra-virgin olive oil
½ teaspoon sweet paprika
½ teaspoon ground cumin
1 teaspoon dried oregano
salt and black pepper, to taste

Spiced mayo

¼ cup (60 g) Whole-egg mayonnaise (page 202) or store-bought mayo
¼ cup (70 g) yoghurt of your choice
½ teaspoon sweet paprika
½ teaspoon ground cumin
½ teaspoon garlic-infused olive oil

To serve

1 tomato, finely diced
1 ripe avocado (¼ per serve, if tolerated), diced or mashed with some salt
1 cup (200 g) tinned or frozen corn kernels
lime wedges, to serve (optional)

This recipe is perfect for busy weeknights when you want a wholesome, flavoursome meal without the fuss. Juicy, tender chicken thighs are seasoned to perfection and cooked with lemon, which infuses a bright, tangy flavour. I love to serve it with rice or quinoa, but it can really be served with any pasta or grain you like.

One-pan lemon and olive chicken

Prep time: 5 minutes
Cook time: 25 minutes
Serves: 4

2 tablespoons extra-virgin
    olive oil
500 g (1 lb 2 oz) skinless,
    boneless chicken thighs
½ teaspoon salt
¼ teaspoon black pepper
1 tablespoon garlic-infused
    olive oil
1 cup (250 ml) water or
    Low-FODMAP chicken stock
    (page 217)
1 low-FODMAP chicken stock
    cube (omit if using chicken
    stock)
1 teaspoon dried chives
1 teaspoon dried oregano
¼ cup (60 ml) milk of your
    choice
½ lemon, sliced into 5mm (¼ in)
    thick rounds
1 tablespoon soft brown sugar
¼ cup (45 g) whole green olives
¼ teaspoon ground cumin
1½ tablespoons cornflour
    (cornstarch) mixed with
    ¼ cup (60 ml) cold water
    (see Tip, page 20)
fresh flat-leaf (Italian) parsley,
    to garnish (optional)

Preheat the oven to 180°C (350°F).

Heat the oil in a deep, ovenproof frying pan (see Tip) over medium–high heat and brown the chicken with the salt and pepper. Once browned, add all the other ingredients, except the parsley, to the pan and cover with the lid or aluminium foil. Bake for 20 minutes.

Serve with your choice of cooked pasta or grains and top with parsley, if you like. Enjoy straight away or store in the fridge for up to 3 days, or in portions in the freezer for up to 3 months.

For the best results, allow to thaw overnight in the fridge, then heat in the microwave for 2–3 minutes, stirring halfway through, until evenly heated. You can also reheat it from frozen in the microwave for 4–6 minutes.

Tip: If you don't have an ovenproof frying pan, simply brown the chicken in a regular frying pan, then transfer to an ovenproof dish or roasting tin.

Don't be put off by making your own pastry; it's actually easier than you think. The best part about this dish is that it doesn't need to be perfect. Got some holes in the pastry? Good! That makes for extra caramelisation and crunch. Doesn't look picture perfect? Who cares! The proof of the pudding is in the eating, as they say.

Easy chicken pot pie

Prep time: 5 minutes
Cook time: 50 minutes
Serves: 4

Filling
¼ cup (60 ml) garlic-infused olive oil

200 g (7 oz) carrot, diced

140 g (5 oz) green beans, diced

100 g (3½ oz) broccoli florets

1 tablespoon dried oregano

1 tablespoon dried basil

½ teaspoon salt, plus extra to serve

2 teaspoons dried chives

½ cup (130 g) sour cream or lactose or dairy-free alternative

1½ cups (375 ml) water or Low-FODMAP chicken stock (page 217)

2 low-FODMAP chicken stock cubes (omit if using chicken stock)

1 tablespoon cornflour (cornstarch) mixed with 2 tablespoons water (see Tip, page 20)

300 g (10½ oz) cooked shredded chicken breast or raw chicken

Pastry (see Tip)
100 g (3½ oz) butter or dairy-free alternative, at room temperature

140 g (5 oz) plain (all-purpose) flour

milk of your choice, or egg wash, for brushing

Preheat the oven to 180°C (350°F).

To make the filling, heat the garlic oil in a saucepan and sauté the carrot over medium–high heat until it begins to soften, about 5 minutes. Add the green beans and broccoli and sauté for another 3–4 minutes.

Next, add all the remaining ingredients, except the shredded chicken, and bring to the boil, then reduce the heat and simmer for 10 minutes. Add the shredded chicken and simmer for another 5–10 minutes until the mixture has thickened.

While the filling is simmering, make the pastry by adding the butter and flour to a bowl with ¼ cup (60 ml). Mix until a soft dough forms. You can do this in a stand mixer fitted with the paddle attachment (start slow and increase the speed as needed) or by hand.

Divide the filling between four individual ovenproof ramekins or pour into a 20 cm (8 in) round pie tin.

If you're making individual pies, divide the pastry into four equal portions and roll into rounds big enough to cover the ramekins (you may have some pastry left over). If you're making one large pie, roll the pastry out into one large round to cover the filling. If your pastry tears while you're placing it on top, don't worry; some gaps are okay, and they can add some nice texture.

Brush the pastry with the milk or egg wash and bake for 20 minutes, or until the pastry is golden. Scatter some extra salt on top of the pastry just before serving, if you like.

Tip: Feel free to replace the pastry with 2 sheets of store-bought gluten-free puff pastry, or even wheat pastry (if you can tolerate it) for an even easier meal.

I bet you didn't know it was this easy to make chicken enchiladas! If you're using leftover chicken, it's even easier. The hardest part is making the sauce, which comes together in only 15 minutes.

Simple chicken enchiladas with Mexican-style rice

Prep time: 10 minutes
Cook time: 55 minutes
Serves: 4

8 corn tortillas

Sauce
¼ cup (60 ml) extra-virgin
    olive oil
3 tablespoons gluten-free plain
    (all-purpose) flour
2 teaspoons ground cumin
2 teaspoons dried oregano
½ teaspoon ground cinnamon
½ teaspoon chilli powder
    (optional)
1 teaspoon salt
4 cups (1 litre) Low-FODMAP
    chicken stock (page 217)
3 tablespoons tomato paste
    (concentrated purée)

Filling
300 g (10½ oz) cooked shredded
    chicken or raw chicken,
    cooked and shredded
½ tablespoon sweet paprika
2 teaspoons dried chives
1 teaspoon ground cumin
1 teaspoon dried oregano
¼ teaspoon smoked paprika
½ teaspoon ground coriander
¼ teaspoon salt
1 cup (245 g) lactose or
    dairy-free sour cream
2 cups (200 g) grated lactose
    or dairy-free cheese

Preheat the oven to 190°C (375°F).

To make the sauce, heat the oil in a saucepan, then add the flour, spices and salt and cook for 1–2 minutes. Add the stock and tomato paste and bring to the boil, then reduce the heat and simmer for 5–10 minutes until thickened.

While the sauce is simmering, combine all the filling ingredients, except half the grated cheese, in a bowl and mix well.

Once the sauce is cooked, spread about ¼ cup (60 ml) of it in the base of a baking dish.

Fill each tortilla with ⅓ cup (80 g) of the filling. Roll up the tortillas and place, seam side down, in the baking dish. Top the rolled-up tortillas with the remaining sauce, then sprinkle the remaining grated cheese over the top. Bake for 20 minutes or until the cheese has melted.

For the rice, mix the passata, stock, ½ cup (125 ml) water, cumin and ground coriander in a bowl.

Heat the garlic oil in a saucepan over medium heat, then add the rice and toast for 2–3 minutes until slightly browned. Add the tomato mixture, then bring to the boil over high heat. Once boiling, reduce the heat to low, cover and simmer for 20 minutes, or until the liquid is absorbed and the rice is cooked. Remove from the heat and allow to cool slightly, then add the coriander leaves and a squeeze of lime (if using) and adjust the seasoning to taste. Fluff with a fork to combine.

Enjoy straight away or store in the fridge for up to 3–4 days or in portions in the freezer for up to 3 months.

For the best results, allow to thaw overnight in the fridge, then heat in the microwave for 2–3 minutes, stirring halfway through, until evenly heated. You can also reheat it from frozen in the microwave for 4–6 minutes.

Rice

1 cup (250 ml) tomato passata
(puréed tomatoes)

1 cup (250 ml) Low-FODMAP
chicken stock (page 217)

½ teaspoon ground cumin

¼ teaspoon ground coriander

2 tablespoons garlic-infused
olive oil

1 cup (200 g) long-grain white
rice, rinsed and drained

2–3 tablespoons fresh coriander
(cilantro) leaves, shredded
(optional)

lime wedges, to serve (optional)

salt and black pepper, to taste

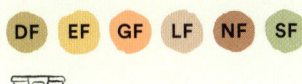

This dish is a one-pot wonder with hints of cinnamon and cumin, and smoky undertones from the paprika. Plus, it is packed with veggies and has an extra boost of fibre from the tinned lentils (see Tip).

One-pot Middle Eastern chicken pilaf

Prep time: 10 minutes
Cook time: 40 minutes
Serves: 4

30 ml (1 fl oz) garlic-infused olive oil
400 g (14 oz) skinless, boneless chicken thighs, cut into 2 cm (¾ in) cubes
160 g (5¾ oz) carrot, cut into 1 cm (½ in) dice
200 g (7 oz) potato, cut into 1 cm (½ in) dice
120 g (4½ oz) red capsicum (pepper), cut into 1 cm (½ in) dice
100 g (3½ oz) green capsicum (pepper), cut into 1 cm (½ in) dice
¼ teaspoon smoked paprika
¼ teaspoon ground cinnamon
½ teaspoon ground cumin
¼ teaspoon cumin seeds
½ teaspoon ground turmeric
½ teaspoon salt
¼ teaspoon black pepper
1 teaspoon lemon juice
160 g (5¾ oz) long-grain white rice, washed and drained
1½ cups (375 ml) water or Low-FODMAP chicken stock (page 217)
2 low-FODMAP chicken stock cubes (omit if using chicken stock)
1 cup (200 g) tinned lentils, drained and rinsed (see Tip)
lemon wedges, to serve (optional)

Heat the garlic oil in a stockpot over medium–high heat and brown the chicken, then add the carrot and potato and cook for 3–4 minutes. Add the remaining vegetables and the spices, salt, pepper and lemon juice and cook for 2 minutes until the spices are fragrant. Next, add the rice, stir through, then add the water and stock cubes (or chicken stock) and the lentils.

Bring to the boil, then cover with a lid, reduce the heat and simmer until the rice is cooked through, stirring occasionally to prevent the rice from sticking, about 20–25 minutes. Once cooked, fluff the rice gently with a fork.

Enjoy straight away or store in the fridge for up to 3–4 days or in portions in the freezer for up to 3 months.

For the best results, allow to thaw overnight in the fridge, then heat in the microwave for 2–3 minutes, stirring halfway through until evenly heated. You can also reheat it from frozen in the microwave for 4–6 minutes.

Serve with a squeeze of lemon, if desired.

Tip: Feel free to omit the lentils if you can't tolerate them, or you can substitute them for tinned chickpeas if you prefer.

This was another nostalgic meal from my childhood that I simply had to make low FODMAP! I truly love anything slow cooked, and this is no exception. The flavours are simple, but the impact is strong. Serve with white rice.

Kokkinisto
Greek chicken stew with white rice

Prep time: 10 minutes
Cook time: 45 minutes
Serves: 4

1 tablespoon extra-virgin olive oil
300 g (10½ oz) skinless,
   boneless chicken thighs, cut
   into 3 cm (1¼ in) dice
1 teaspoon salt
¼ teaspoon black pepper
2 tablespoons garlic-infused
   olive oil
2 low-FODMAP chicken
   stock cubes
1 teaspoon dried basil
1 teaspoon dried oregano
1 teaspoon dried parsley
1 teaspoon dried chives
450 g (1 lb) tinned tomatoes
140 g (5 oz) carrot, cut into 2 cm
   (¾ in) half-moons
230 g (8 oz) potato, cut into
   2–3 cm (¾–1¼ in) chunks
1 cup (200 g) long-grain
   white rice, rinsed and drained

Heat the extra-virgin olive oil in a stockpot over medium–high heat and brown the chicken with the salt and pepper for 3–4 minutes. Once the chicken is browned, add all the remaining ingredients, except the carrot, potato and rice, with 1 cup (250 ml) water. Bring to the boil, then reduce the heat to medium–low and simmer for 10 minutes until the stew has slightly thickened. Add the carrot and potato and simmer for another 20–30 minutes until the vegetables are cooked through.

In the meantime, bring a saucepan of water to the boil and cook the rice according to the packet instructions until al dente, then drain.

Serve the stew over the rice.

This chapter is dedicated to quick, delicious and satisfying recipes that bring the best of meat to your table with minimal effort. Thankfully, proteins such as red meat, poultry and fish are naturally low FODMAP. Red meat is also packed with iron and essential B vitamins, making it a powerhouse of flavour and nourishment. Whether you're juggling a busy schedule or simply looking for straightforward yet mouthwatering meals, this chapter provides a variety of recipes designed to make your cooking experience as enjoyable and stress free as possible.

Easy Meals

With Meat

Straight from my yiayia's kitchen (with some low-FODMAP tweaks), this is a dish I associate with comfort and nostalgia. Those who dined at our cafe in the early days will remember seeing this on the menu. The roasted vegetables pair so well with the lamb, and the creamy béchamel sauce adds such richness that you will keep coming back for more. I guarantee if you make this for your next dinner party, no one will notice it is gluten free and low FODMAP.

Moussaka

Prep time: 2 hours
Cook time: 45 minutes
Serves: 8–10

700 g (1 lb 9 oz) potatoes, peeled, cut into 5 mm–1 cm (¼–½ in) thick rounds
600 g (1 lb 5 oz) zucchini (courgette), halved lengthways, cut into 5 mm–1 cm (¼–½ in) thick strips
900 g (2 lb) eggplant (aubergine), cut into 5 mm–1 cm (¼–½ in) thick rounds
¼ cup (60 ml) extra-virgin olive oil
salt and black pepper

Mince

1 kg (2 lb 4 oz) minced (ground) lamb
1 tablespoon dried oregano
1 low-FODMAP beef stock cube
1 tablespoon garlic-infused olive oil
1 teaspoon salt
1 × 400 g (14 oz) tin tomatoes
1 tablespoon dried chives
½ teaspoon black pepper
3 teaspoons dried basil

Preheat the oven to 180°C (350°F).

Place the potato, zucchini and eggplant on three separate baking trays and roast for 20–25 minutes, or until cooked through. If you have a barbecue, you can also grill the vegetables, which gives an extra depth of flavour.

Oil the base of a 33 × 23 × 5 cm (13 × 9 × 2 in) rectangular baking dish, or a round baking dish of a similar size, and make a layer of potato in the bottom, making sure there are no holes or gaps (you will need to cut some of the potato to make sure every inch is covered). Next, do the same with the zucchini and then the eggplant, ensuring there are no holes or gaps in the layers. Set aside.

To make the mince, brown the minced lamb in a stockpot over medium–high heat until no longer pink, about 10–15 minutes. Once the meat is browned, add all the remaining ingredients and bring to the boil. Reduce the heat to low and simmer for 45–60 minutes. Allow the meat to cool slightly, then spread it in an even layer over the vegetables.

Preheat the oven to 180°C (350°F).

For the béchamel (see page 84), heat the oils in a large saucepan over high heat for 2 minutes. Add the cornflour and whisk for 2 minutes, making sure to stir the side of the pot so it doesn't stick or burn. Slowly add the milk, whisking constantly, until it comes to the boil. This might take some time, but don't worry; it will suddenly begin to thicken. The main thing is to continue to whisk to prevent it from sticking and burning. Once thickened, add the salt, pepper and cheese, and turn off the heat. Continue stirring until all the cheese has melted, then remove from the heat. Allow to cool for 10 minutes or so, then pour on top of the meat.

Bake the moussaka for 40–45 minutes until the top of the béchamel is nice and brown.

Cool for 15 minutes before serving to allow the béchamel to thicken up a little, or it will be too runny when you cut it.

→

Béchamel (see Tips)

⅓ cup (80 ml) extra-virgin
    olive oil
1 tablespoon canola or
    vegetable oil
65 g (2½ oz) cornflour
    (cornstarch)
4 cups (1 litre) milk of your choice
1 teaspoon salt
pinch of black pepper
50 g (1¾ oz) cheddar or
    mozzarella cheese, or lactose
    or dairy-free cheese of your
    choice, grated

Tips: This dish tastes even better the next day, much like a bolognese, as the flavours have more time to develop, so please feel free to make it a day ahead and leave the last step until the day of serving. Just remember to bring it out of the fridge about 30 minutes before cooking.

If you are dairy free, you can use plant milk for the béchamel sauce. However, the moussaka does taste best with cow's milk, so if you are lactose free, I recommend using a lactose-free milk over a soy or almond milk. You may also need to add more cornflour if using plant milk, as it is thinner and might not thicken as well.

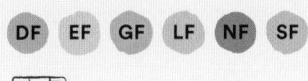

This is one of my favourite meals, particularly on a cold winter's day. There is something so comforting about slow-cooked meals. They're always my go-to when I need an energy boost, and they're great for prepping ahead. The umami richness of this stew will surprise you and will prove to any sceptic that low-FODMAP recipes can have the same depth of flavour as any other dish.

Warming beef stew

Prep time: 10 minutes
Cook time: 1 hour 30 minutes
Serves: 4

550 g (1 lb 4 oz) beef chuck, cut into 3–4 cm (1¼–1½ in) chunks
15 g (½ oz) cornflour (cornstarch) mixed with 1 tablespoon water (see page 20)
½ teaspoon salt, plus extra for seasoning
½ teaspoon black pepper, plus extra for seasoning
2 tablespoons garlic-infused olive oil
2 cup (500 ml) water or Low-FODMAP beef stock (page 215)
3 low-FODMAP beef stock cubes (omit if using beef stock)
2 teaspoons dried chives
1 teaspoon dried rosemary
⅓ cup (80 ml) red wine
40 g (1½ oz) tomato paste (concentrated purée)
400 g (14 oz) carrot, cut into 2 cm (¾ in) dice
400 g (14 oz) potato, cut into 2 cm (¾ in) dice

Coat the beef with the cornflour, salt and pepper.

Heat the garlic oil in a stockpot over medium–high heat and sear the beef until well browned. You might need to do this in batches, depending on the size of your pot, so as not to overcrowd the pan.

Once the beef is browned, add all the other ingredients, except the carrot and potato, and bring to the boil, making sure to scrape the bottom of the pot to loosen any stuck-on bits. Reduce the heat to a simmer and cook for 45 minutes.

Add the carrot and simmer for another 10 minutes before adding the potato. Continue to simmer for another 30–40 minutes until the beef is tender and the vegetables are cooked through. If it looks a little dry, add some water. Taste and adjust the seasoning if necessary before serving.

Serve immediately or store in the fridge for up to 3–4 days or in portions in the freezer for up to 3 months.

For the best results, allow to thaw overnight in the fridge, then heat in the microwave for 2–3 minutes, stirring halfway through, until evenly heated. You can also reheat it from frozen in the microwave for 4–6 minutes.

I've made this dish as an appetiser for countless parties, and it never fails to steal the show. The tender, perfectly spiced koftas pair so beautifully with the cool, creamy minted yoghurt that each bite feels like a burst of flavour in your mouth. It's one of those dishes that has everyone coming back for seconds. And the best part? No one ever realises it's low FODMAP! So, let's keep this secret between us.

Beef koftas with pita bread and minted yoghurt

Prep time: 20 minutes
Cook time: 20 minutes
Serves: 4

lemon wedges, to serve

Koftas
500 g (1 lb 2 oz) minced (ground) beef
1 teaspoon sweet paprika
¼ cup (15 g) chopped fresh mint
¼ cup (15 g) chopped fresh flat-leaf (Italian) parsley
1 tablespoon Napoli sauce (page 214) or tomato paste (concentrated purée)
½ teaspoon salt
½ teaspoon ground cumin
½ teaspoon ground cinnamon
¼ teaspoon ground allspice
1 egg

Pita breads
250 g (9 oz) plain (all-purpose) flour of your choice (see Tips)
2 teaspoons baking powder
½ teaspoon salt
1 teaspoon xanthan gum (omit if using regular flour)
2½ tablespoons canola oil

Minted yoghurt
2 tablespoons chopped fresh mint, plus extra shredded mint to serve
½ cup (130 g) yoghurt of your choice (see Tips)
1–2 teaspoons sugar (optional)

Preheat the oven to 180°C (350°F).

In a large bowl, combine all the ingredients for the koftas and mix until well combined. You can do this by hand or using a stand mixer fitted with the paddle attachment – just be sure to use low speed to avoid overmixing. Form the mixture into large balls of approximately 1 heaped tablespoon per ball (see Tips). Place the koftas on a baking tray lined with baking paper. Bake for 15–20 minutes until cooked through.

For the pita bread, combine all the ingredients, except the oil, in a bowl. Add the oil with ¾ cup (185 ml) water and mix until combined. Divide the dough into four equal portions and roll into balls. If you're using regular wheat flour, rest the dough for about 30 minutes before rolling the balls out into discs about 1 cm (½ in) thick.

Heat a dry, non-stick frying pan over medium heat and fry the pita breads, one by one, for 1–2 minutes on each side until golden brown.

Finally, to make the minted yoghurt, add the mint to the yoghurt with the sugar (if using) and mix well to combine.

Serve the koftas inside the warm bread, topped with some minted yoghurt, extra shredded mint and a squeeze of lemon.

Tips: I have made these pita breads using both gluten-free and regular flour, and they work well either way, so use whatever you have on hand or can tolerate.

Use whatever yoghurt you like, but this recipe does work best with dairy as opposed to non-dairy yoghurt, as non-dairy yoghurts have a different and often stronger flavour than regular cow's milk yoghurt. If you aren't dairy free, I recommend using regular or lactose-free yoghurt.

You can make the koftas into smaller, bite-sized balls and take them to parties as an appetiser with the minted yoghurt as a dipping sauce.

This dish is full of flavour and comes together in no time. A little sweet, a little salty, it will have your tastebuds singing and will quickly become a go-to dish. You can customise it as you wish: add less sugar, more chilli, whatever you like. Work with it until you find your sweet spot. Personally, I'm a wimp with spice, so I prefer it a little sweeter.

Korean beef with rice

Prep time: 5 minutes
Cook time: 30 minutes
Serves: 4

500 g (1 lb 2 oz) minced
   (ground) beef
130 g (4½ oz) red capsicum
   (pepper), cut into 1 cm (½ in)
   thick strips
130 g (4½ oz) green capsicum
   (pepper), cut into 1 cm (½ in)
   thick strips
100 g (3½ oz) carrot, cut into
   half-moons approx. 1 cm
   (½ in) thick
1 cup (200 g) long-grain white
   rice, rinsed and drained
toasted sesame seeds, to garnish
finely sliced spring onion
   (scallion), to garnish
dried chives, to garnish
   (optional)

Sauce
15 g (½ oz) soft brown sugar
120 ml (4 fl oz) soy sauce
2 tablespoons dried chives
½ teaspoons minced ginger
½ teaspoon chilli flakes
   (optional)
1½ tablespoons garlic-infused
   olive oil
15 ml (½ fl oz) sesame oil

Combine all the sauce ingredients in a bowl and mix well.

Place a frying pan over high heat and fry the mince until cooked through and no longer pink, about 4–5 minutes. Once cooked, add the sauce and bring the mixture to the boil. Add the vegetables and reduce the heat to medium–low. Simmer for 15–20 minutes or until the vegetables are cooked through.

While the vegetables are cooking, bring a saucepan of water to the boil and cook the rice according to the packet instructions or until al dente.

Serve the rice with the Korean beef and vegetables, garnished with sesame seeds, spring onion and dried chives, if using. Enjoy straight away or store in the fridge for 3–4 days or in portions in the freezer for up to 3 months.

For the best results, allow the soup to thaw overnight in the fridge and heat in the microwave for 2–3 minutes, stirring halfway through, until evenly heated. You can also reheat it from frozen in the microwave for 4–6 minutes.

DF EF GF LF NF SF

This pulled beef is so very easy to make, especially on the weekend when I have a little more time, as it takes over 4 hours to cook. In fact, I make it almost weekly and keep frozen portions to use in salads, wraps or burgers throughout the week. It's very convenient to have on hand for a quick, tasty meal. It's best to make the slaw a few hours ahead to allow the carrot and fennel to pickle in the liquid. Refrigerate until ready to serve.

Pulled beef burger with carrot fennel slaw

Prep time: 15 minutes
Cook time: 4 hours 30 minutes
Serves: 6–8

Pulled beef
2 tablespoons garlic-infused
    olive oil or extra-virgin olive oil
1 kg (2 lb 4 oz) beef chuck, cut
    into chunks (see Tip)
2 carrots, cut into large dice
300 ml (10½ fl oz) red wine or
    600 ml (21 fl oz) Low-FODMAP
    beef stock (page 215)
300 ml (10½ fl oz) water
1 tablespoon dried thyme
3 teaspoons dried rosemary
1 teaspoon salt

Slaw
200 g (7 oz) carrot, grated
80 g (2¾ oz) fennel, cut into thin
    matchsticks
2 teaspoons dried chives
1 teaspoon salt
½ teaspoon black pepper
¼ cup (60 ml) extra-virgin
    olive oil
2 tablespoons white vinegar

To serve
burger buns of your choice
Maple dijon mayonnaise
    (page 202)
cheese of your choice (optional)
bacon (optional)
lettuce (optional)

For the pulled beef, heat the garlic oil in a large saucepan over high heat. Add the beef and sear until all sides are well browned (you may need to work in batches). Once the beef is browned, add all the remaining ingredients and bring to the boil. Once boiling, reduce the heat to low, cover with a lid and simmer for 3–4 hours, or until the meat is very tender and breaks apart with a fork.

Gently remove the meat and carrot from the pan, increase the heat to high and simmer for another 20–30 minutes, or until the liquid has reduced by half.

While the liquid is simmering, shred the beef and carrot into a bowl using two forks.

Pour the reduced liquid onto the pulled beef and carrot slowly, adding as much as you want. Set aside until ready to serve.

Combine all the slaw ingredients in a bowl and mix well.

Serve straight away or store the pulled beef in the fridge for 3–4 days, or in portions in the freezer for up to 3 months.

To assemble your burgers, spread the buns with some of the maple dijon mayo and fill with the beef and slaw. You can add some cheese, bacon and lettuce too if you like, but I quite like these with just the beef and slaw.

For the best results, allow to thaw overnight in the fridge, then heat in the microwave for 2–3 minutes, stirring halfway through, until evenly heated. You can also reheat it from frozen in the microwave for 4–6 minutes.

Tip: I have also made this with diced pork chops (using stock instead of wine), so this recipe doubles as a pulled pork dish.

Tender, marinated steak bites drizzled with a luxurious, creamy sauce – dinner doesn't come much better than this. This is a deconstructed take on a classic that will soon become a family favourite. And is it just me or does bite-sized anything just taste better?

Steak bowl with caramelised fennel

Prep time: 10 minutes, plus marinating
Cook time: 30–40 minutes
Serves: 4

1 kg (2 lb 4 oz) sirloin steak, or your favourite cut, sliced into bite-sized strips approx. 5 cm (2 in) in length
2 tablespoons extra-virgin olive oil

Steak marinade
2 tablespoons extra-virgin olive oil
2 teaspoons dried basil
2 teaspoons dried oregano
2 tablespoons garlic-infused olive oil
2 teaspoons lemon juice
3 teaspoons balsamic vinegar
2 tablespoons chopped fresh flat-leaf (Italian) parsley
½ teaspoon salt
¼ teaspoon black pepper

Sauce
3 teaspoons dijon mustard
½ teaspoon dried or fresh chopped rosemary
¾ cup (185 ml) milk of your choice
1 tablespoon extra-virgin olive oil
1 tablespoon garlic-infused olive oil
½ teaspoon salt
¼ teaspoon black pepper
3 teaspoons cornflour (cornstarch) mixed with 2 teaspoons water (see Tip, page 20)

Combine all the marinade ingredients in a bowl. Add the sliced steak and refrigerate to marinate for 1–2 hours.

Heat the oil in a frying pan over high heat for 1–2 minutes until the oil is hot. Add the marinated steak and reduce the heat to medium–high. Cook for 2 minutes on each side, or until cooked to your liking. The meat should get a nice char on the outside. Remove the steak from the pan and cover lightly with aluminium foil to rest. Turn the heat down to medium–low.

Remove any burnt-on bits from the frying pan (reserving the steak juices, as they will add extra flavour), then add all the sauce ingredients along with the reserved juices. Cook the sauce for 3–4 minutes, stirring regularly so it doesn't burn, until thickened. Keep warm until you're ready to serve.

For the vegetables, preheat the oven to 180°C (350°F).

Roasted vegetables

400 g (14 oz) potatoes, peeled
  and cut into 2 cm (¾ in) dice
200 g (7 oz) carrots, peeled and
  cut into 2 cm (¾ in) dice
¼ cup (60 ml) extra-virgin
  olive oil
3 teaspoons dried oregano
¼ teaspoon black pepper
½ teaspoon sweet paprika
1 teaspoon salt
200 g (7 oz/3⅓ cups) broccoli
  florets

Caramelised fennel

160 g (5¾ oz/approx. 1 small)
  fennel bulb
1 tablespoon extra-virgin olive oil
pinch of salt and black pepper

Put the potato and carrot in a roasting tin with most of the oil, and the herbs and spices, and mix well to coat the vegetables. Bake for 20–30 minutes, turning halfway through, or until cooked through and golden brown.

Drizzle the broccoli with the remaining oil and season with salt and pepper. Add to the roasting tin for the final 10–15 minutes of cooking.

While the vegetables are cooking, cut the fennel bulb in half and remove the core in a wedge shape, then thinly slice.

Heat the oil in a frying pan over medium–low heat, add the fennel and some salt and pepper, and cook for 20–30 minutes until the fennel has softened and is nice and caramelised.

Serve the meat, roasted vegetables and caramelised fennel in a bowl and drizzle generously with the sauce – enjoy!

DF EF GF LF SF

I believe Massaman curry is one of the most underrated Thai dishes. The most complex part is making the curry paste, but this can be frozen, so make double and have it ready to go for the next time you're craving this dish. To make it low FODMAP, I've used spring onion (scallion) tops instead of shallots or onions, along with garlic-infused olive oil.

Massaman curry with white rice

Prep time: 10 minutes
Cook time: 1 hour 30 minutes
Serves: 4

500 g (1 lb 2 oz) beef chuck, cut into 2 cm (¾ in) thick strips (see Tip)
3 teaspoons cornflour (cornstarch)
2 tablespoons canola oil or other neutral-flavoured oil
1 cup (250 ml) water or Low-FODMAP beef stock (page 215)
1 low-FODMAP beef stock cube (omit if using beef stock)
160 ml (5¼ fl oz) coconut cream
400 g (14 oz) potatoes, peeled and cut into 3 cm (1¼ in) dice
salt and black pepper
peanuts, to garnish
cooked white rice, to serve

Paste

½ lemongrass stalk, cleaned
15 g (½ oz/½ cup, loosely packed) fresh coriander (cilantro) stems and leaves
1 medium red chilli
1½ tablespoons garlic-infused olive oil
1 teaspoon each ground coriander, ground cumin and soft brown sugar
½ teaspoon each ground cinnamon, ground cardamom, ground nutmeg, minced ginger and fish sauce
¼ teaspoon each ground white pepper and salt
⅛ teaspoon ground cloves
⅛ cup (15 g) chopped spring onion (scallion), green part only

For the paste, bruise the lemongrass stalk by pressing it with the flat side of a knife. Combine all the ingredients in a bowl and purée with a hand-held blender until a smooth paste forms. You can also do this with a mortar and pestle or in a high-speed blender.

Coat the beef strips in the cornflour and season generously with salt and pepper.

Heat the oil in a large saucepan over medium–high heat and brown the beef for 3–4 minutes. Once the beef is browned, reduce the heat to medium and add the paste. Cook for 2 minutes or until fragrant. Add the water and stock cube (or beef stock) and the coconut cream. Bring to the boil, then turn the heat down to low and simmer for 30–40 minutes, or until the beef is tender. Make sure to scrape the bottom of the pan to loosen any stuck-on bits and stir occasionally to prevent burning or further sticking.

Finally, add the potato and cook for another 20–30 minutes or until the potato is cooked through.

Serve immediately with white rice or store in the fridge for 3–4 days or in portions in the freezer for up to 3 months.

For the best results, allow to thaw overnight in the fridge, then heat in the microwave for 2–3 minutes, stirring halfway through, until evenly heated. You can also reheat it from frozen in the microwave for 4–6 minutes.

Tip: I like to cut the beef into strips as opposed to the traditional chunks so that it cooks faster. Feel free to cut into chunks if you prefer, but it will take a bit longer to cook, about 30–45 minutes.

DF EF GF LF NF SF

Is there anything better (or more low-maintenance) than a roast? Simply season the lamb generously, throw it in the oven and walk away. Just over an hour and a half later, you have a delicious dinner ready to devour. But the real winner here is the gravy – using the pan juices means the flavour is simply unmatched.

Roast lamb with potatoes, carrot and gravy

Prep time: 10 minutes
Cook time: 1 hour 40 minutes
Serves: 6–8

1.5 kg (3 lb 5 oz) boneless leg of lamb (see Tips)
2 tablespoons extra-virgin olive oil
1 tablespoon salt
1 tablespoon dijon mustard
¾ tablespoon dried rosemary
½ tablespoon dried thyme
800 g (1 lb 12 oz) small-to-medium potatoes
350 g (12 oz) carrots
1–2 cups (250–500 ml) water or Low-FODMAP beef stock (page 215)
1–2 low-FODMAP beef stock cubes (omit if using beef stock)
1 tablespoon cornflour (cornstarch)

Line a roasting tin with aluminium foil and preheat the oven to 180°C (350°F).

Place the lamb in the lined tin and prick the meat 15–20 times with a sharp knife. This will help the flavours seep into the meat while cooking. Rub 1 tablespoon of the oil on the top of the lamb, then flip it over and rub the other tablespoon on the bottom. Sprinkle generously all over with the salt, then smear with the dijon mustard so that it is well coated. Scatter the rosemary and thyme on top, being sure to flip the lamb to ensure it is seasoned on all sides.

Peel and cut the potatoes into quarters. Peel and cut the carrots into thirds lengthways. Add the potato and carrot to the tin around the lamb and cook for 1 hour 30 minutes until the vegetables and meat are cooked to your liking (see Tips). Remove from the oven, transfer the vegetables to a separate bowl or plate and cover with aluminium foil to keep warm. Place the lamb on a chopping board, cover lightly with foil and allow to rest while you make the gravy.

To make the gravy, carefully pour the juices from the tin into a small saucepan, scraping to remove the charred bits (this is extra flavour). Depending on how much juice is in the tray, add 1–2 cups (250–500 ml) water and the beef stock cubes (or beef stock). Stir to combine, then place over medium–high heat and add the cornflour. Whisk to dissolve the cornflour, stirring continuously until the gravy is thick, 5–10 minutes.

Slice the meat and serve with the gravy and vegetables. You can eat this straight away or store in the fridge for 3–4 days, or in portions in the freezer for up to 3 months.

For the best results, allow to thaw overnight in the fridge, then heat in the microwave for 2–3 minutes, stirring halfway through, until evenly heated. You can also reheat it from frozen in the microwave for 4–6 minutes.

Tips: Start with the lamb at room temperature before roasting, as this will help it cook more evenly.

The general rule for lamb is about 25 minutes per 500 g (1 lb 2 oz) for medium.

DF EF GF LF NF SF

This iconic French dish features tender chunks of beef cooked slowly in a luxurious red-wine sauce infused with the deep, savoury flavours of aromatic vegetables and herbs. Leaving out the traditional ingredients of onion and mushrooms keeps this low FODMAP, but it's just as tasty and satisfying.

Rich beef bourguignon with mashed potatoes

Prep time: 10 minutes
Cook time: 1 hour 40 minutes
Serves: 4–6

2 tablespoons extra-virgin
   olive oil
750 g (1 lb 10 oz) beef chuck, cut
   into 4–5 cm (1½–2 in) chunks
300 ml (10½ fl oz) red wine
1½ low-FODMAP beef stock
   cubes
1 teaspoon soft brown sugar
1 teaspoon dried thyme
2 teaspoons dried parsley
1 teaspoon sweet paprika
1 bay leaf
1 tablespoon dried chives
1 teaspoon salt
¼ teaspoon black pepper
40 g (1½ oz) tomato paste
   (concentrated purée)
1½ tablespoons garlic-infused
   olive oil
200 g (7 oz) carrot, peeled and
   cut into 2–3 cm (¾–1¼ in)
   thick rounds
200 g (7 oz) potato, peeled and
   cut into 3 cm (1¼ in) chunks
2½ tablespoons cornflour
   (cornstarch) mixed with ¼ cup
   (60 ml) cold water (see Tip,
   page 20)
flat-leaf (Italian) parsley, to
   garnish (optional)

Heat the oil in a stockpot or large saucepan over medium–high heat, add the beef and brown on all sides for about 5 minutes. Add the wine, 300 ml (10½ fl oz) water and stock cubes with the brown sugar, herbs and spices, tomato paste and garlic oil. Bring to the boil, then reduce the heat to low, cover with a lid and simmer for 45 minutes to 1 hour, or until the meat is tender, stirring occasionally to prevent it from sticking.

Add the carrot and potato and simmer for another 30–40 minutes until the vegetables are cooked through. Add the cornflour slurry and continue to simmer until the stew has thickened.

While the carrot and potato are cooking, place the potato for the mash in another stockpot and cover with cold water. Season generously with salt and bring to a rapid boil over high heat. Reduce the heat slightly if it starts to boil over, but keep it at a rapid boil. Cook for 20–25 minutes, or until a potato is easily crushed with a fork against the side of the pot. Drain, then mash the potato with a potato masher. Add the butter and milk and mash again until combined. Taste and adjust the seasoning to your liking.

Serve the mashed potato topped with the beef bourguignon. Scatter some fresh parsley on top to garnish. Enjoy straight away or store in the fridge for 3–4 days or in portions in the freezer for up to 3 months.

For the best results, allow to thaw overnight in the fridge, then heat in the microwave for 2–3 minutes, stirring halfway through, until evenly heated. You can also reheat it from frozen in the microwave for 4–6 minutes.

Mashed potato

1 kg (2 lb 4 oz) potato, peeled
    and cut into 1–2 cm (½–¾ in)
    cubes
25 g (1 oz) butter or dairy-free
    alternative
¼ cup (60 ml) milk of your
    choice
salt and pepper, to taste

With tender lamb, crunchy pita chips and a fresh, herby salad, this dish is truly a winner. Every mouthful is an explosion of flavour and texture. Wow your friends at your next gathering with this recipe – it definitely won't disappoint.

Lamb backstrap with fattoush salad

Prep time: 5 minutes, plus marinating
Cook time: 10–15 minutes
Serves: 4

500 g (1 lb 2 oz) lamb backstrap
2 pita breads (store bought or homemade; see page 86)
250 g (9 oz) cherry tomatoes, halved
2¾ cups (100 g) rocket (arugula)
½ cup (10 g) flat-leaf (Italian) parsley
⅓ cup (20 g) mint leaves
¼–½ quantity Tzatziki (pages 146–7), plus extra to serve

Lamb marinade
½ tablespoon ground cumin
½ tablespoon sweet paprika
½ teaspoon salt
2 teaspoons chopped fresh coriander (cilantro) leaves
2 teaspoons chopped flat-leaf (Italian) parsley leaves
2 teaspoons lemon juice
1 tablespoon garlic-infused olive oil
1 tablespoon extra-virgin olive oil

Combine the marinade ingredients in a large bowl. Add the lamb backstrap and marinate for 1–2 hours in the fridge.

Preheat the oven to 200°C (400°F). Line a baking tray with baking paper and cut the pita breads into triangles. Spread the bread out on the tray, spray with olive oil and bake for 5 minutes, or until crisp, turning halfway.

Spray a large, non-stick frying pan with olive oil and place over high heat. Add the lamb and cook for 3 minutes on each side, or until cooked to your liking. Alternatively, you can cook the lamb on the barbecue for a fantastic charred flavour. Transfer to a plate, cover lightly with aluminium foil and allow to rest.

Mix the tomato with the rocket, parsley and mint. Add the tzatziki and pita chips and gently toss to combine. Slice the lamb.

Divide the salad between plates and top with the sliced lamb. Drizzle some extra tzatziki on top to serve.

DF EF GF LF NF SF

Unlike traditional chilli con carne, this recipe is packed with vegetables to make it a more well-rounded meal. It's simple and tasty and a favourite weeknight dinner in our house. I have omitted the beans and other high-FODMAP ingredients that typically go into this dish. I've swapped them for extra vegetables to replace the fibre lost by removing the beans. It's great served with brown rice for added nutrients, but you can serve it with any grain or pasta you like, or enjoy it just as it is! I also like to add a dash of sour cream and a sprinkle of cheese on top for a little extra authenticity (lactose- or dairy-free options work, too).

Chilli con carne

Prep time: 5 minutes
Cook time: 45 minutes
Serves: 4

500 g (1 lb 2 oz) minced
   (ground) beef
2 teaspoons garlic-infused
   olive oil
50 g (1¾ oz) carrot, cut into
   1 cm (½ in) dice
2 teaspoons ground cumin
1 teaspoon dried oregano
2 teaspoons sweet paprika
1 teaspoon smoked paprika
1 teaspoon chilli flakes (see Tip)
1 tablespoon dried chives
1 teaspoon salt
½ teaspoon black pepper
1 × 400 g (14 oz) tin tomatoes
15 g (½ oz) tomato paste
   (concentrated purée)
1 low-FODMAP beef stock cube
60 g (2¼ oz) zucchini
   (courgette), cut into 1 cm
   (½ in) dice
50 g (1¾ oz) green capsicum
   (pepper), cut into 1 cm
   (½ in) dice
30 g (1 oz) sweetcorn kernels

Heat a saucepan over high heat and brown the beef for about 5 minutes, or until cooked through and no longer pink. Add the garlic oil, carrot, spices, tinned tomatoes, tomato paste, stock cube and ¼ cup (60 ml) water, then reduce the heat to low and simmer for 10 minutes.

Add the zucchini and green capsicum and simmer for a further 20 minutes. Finally, add the corn and simmer for another 5–10 minutes, or until all the vegetables are cooked to your liking.

Serve straight away with rice or pasta of your choice, or store in the fridge for 3–4 days or in portions in the freezer for up to 3 months.

For the best results, allow to thaw overnight in the fridge, then heat in the microwave for 2–3 minutes, stirring halfway through, until evenly heated. You can also reheat it from frozen in the microwave for 4–6 minutes.

Tip: Feel free to adjust the amount of chilli flakes depending on your preference for heat.

Eating vegetarian can be a challenge with the low-FODMAP diet because there are a lot of vegetables and legumes on the no-go list and portion sizes are very important. Here, I have curated a selection of vegetarian dishes that are more enticing than the usual options out there.

Plant-Powered:

Your Veggie Go-Tos

Bruschetta is traditionally just tomato, onion and garlic but, since onion is not an ingredient used in the low-FODMAP diet, I have added some extra vegetables for a boost of flavour. The addition of labneh takes this up a level and cuts through the sweet roasted capsicum (pepper) with a touch of tang. Labneh is simply hung yoghurt where the water has been drained to create a very thick, soft, cheese-like product. I love having this for brunch or lunch on some toast. You will need to start this recipe one day in advance.

Roasted capsicum and olive bruschetta with labneh

Prep time: 10 minutes, plus draining
Cook time: 35 minutes
Serves: approx. 6

1 red capsicum (pepper)
1 tomato, finely diced
10 g (¼ oz) spring onion (scallion), green top only, finely diced
15–20 pitted kalamata (black) olives, thinly sliced
½ tablespoon finely chopped fresh or dried basil
1 teaspoon balsamic vinegar
½ teaspoon salt
¼ teaspoon black pepper
bread of your choice, bread stick or slices
garlic-infused olive oil, for drizzling

Labneh (see Tip)
½ cup (130 g) yoghurt of your choice

To make the labneh, simply add the yoghurt to a piece of muslin (cheesecloth), or even a clean disposable cloth, and twist it tightly so that the excess liquid can drain out. Place it in a sieve suspended over a bowl with a weight on top and leave it in the fridge to drain for 8 hours or overnight.

Preheat the oven to 220°C (425°F), place the capsicum on a baking tray and roast for 20–30 minutes, or until the skin has blackened. Remove from the oven and transfer the capsicum to a plate or bowl and cover with plastic wrap while still hot. The steam will help loosen the skin, making it easier to peel once cool.

Add the tomato, spring onion and olives to a bowl with the basil, balsamic, salt and pepper.

Once the capsicum has cooled, carefully peel off the skin and remove the seeds from the inside. It should be roasted and soft. Slice very thinly or dice the capsicum and add it to the bowl with the tomato mixture.

Toast or chargrill the bread and drizzle with some garlic oil, then top with the capsicum mix and dollop some labneh on top. If you prefer, you can spread some labneh on the toast first, then top with the bruschetta mix.

Tip: Labneh will last in the fridge for 1–2 weeks so can be made in advance.

There is just something about a colourful salad that makes the eyes widen with delight. This salad is packed with healthy ingredients and has the added benefit of pickled cabbage, which is great for gut health. The cabbage is so easy to make, plus it keeps in the fridge for weeks. Add to salads, wraps, sandwiches, toast and even tacos!

Pickled cabbage and quinoa rainbow salad with miso dressing

Prep time: 10 minutes, plus pickling
Cook time: 25 minutes
Serves: 4

Pickled cabbage

500 g (1 lb 2 oz) red cabbage, core removed
2 cups (500 ml) distilled white vinegar
2 teaspoons lemon juice
2 teaspoons salt
1 tablespoon caster (superfine) sugar
2 teaspoons dijon mustard

Salad

1 cup (200 g) quinoa
300 g (10½ oz) carrot, grated
150 g (5½ oz) tinned diced beetroot (beet), drained
150 g (5½ oz) frozen edamame, thawed
120 g (4¼ oz) Pickled cabbage (see above)
2⅔ cups (160 g) broccoli florets, steamed or boiled
30 g (1 oz) kale, shredded
Miso dressing (page 208), to taste

To make the pickled cabbage, thinly slice the cabbage either by hand or with a mandolin. To a large container with a lid, add all the pickling ingredients and give them a good mix to make sure they are well combined. Add the cabbage and press down in the liquid to make sure it is well submerged. Cover with the lid and refrigerate for at least 2 hours before serving.

Thoroughly rinse the quinoa in a sieve under cold running water. Once rinsed, add to a large saucepan with 2¼ cups (560 ml) water. Bring to the boil over high heat, then reduce the heat to low, cover and simmer for 12–15 minutes, or until the water has evaporated and the quinoa is cooked. Allow to sit for 5–10 minutes, then fluff with a fork.

To make the salad, simply combine all the ingredients, except the dressing, with the cooked quinoa, then dress with the miso dressing. Serve the salad with the pickled cabbage on the side.

The left-over pickled cabbage will keep in an airtight container in the fridge for 2–3 weeks.

You cannot go wrong with a frittata. It is great for a quick, healthy lunch or a light dinner – even a breakfast! This recipe is so simple that all you need is one roasting tin. Simply roast the vegetables and add the egg mix. Bake in the oven and voila! A delicious frittata.

Mediterranean veggie frittata

Prep time: 5 minutes
Cook time: 50 minutes
Serves: 6–8

200 g (7 oz) kabocha (Japanese) pumpkin (squash), skin removed, cut into 2–3 cm (¾–1¼ in) dice

200 g (7 oz) zucchini (courgette), cut into 2–3 cm (¾–1¼ in) dice

200 g (7 oz) red capsicum, cut into 2–3 cm (¾–1¼ in) dice

1 tablespoon extra-virgin olive oil

½ teaspoon salt

¼ teaspoon black pepper

12 eggs

5 cups (1.25 litres) milk of your choice (see Tip)

¼ teaspoon sweet paprika

1 teaspoon dried chives

½ teaspoon dried basil

½ teaspoon dried oregano

1 tomato, cut into 2 cm (¾ in) dice

25 g (1 oz) baby spinach

Preheat the oven to 180°C (350°F).

Add the pumpkin, zucchini and capsicum to a 23 × 33 cm (13 × 9 in) roasting tin or baking dish. Drizzle with the oil, add the salt and pepper, then roast for 10–15 minutes until cooked through.

While the vegetables are roasting, combine the eggs, milk, spices and herbs in a large jug or bowl, and whisk thoroughly until combined.

Once the vegetables are cooked, allow the tin to cool slightly before making sure the vegetables are spread evenly in the tin. Add the tomato and spinach and, finally, pour the egg and milk mixture directly into the tin with the roasted vegetables.

Return to the oven and bake for 25–35 minutes, or until golden brown and a toothpick inserted in the middle comes out clean.

Allow to cool for 10–15 minutes before cutting. Serve as is or with your side salad of choice.

Tip: I have made this with dairy-free milk and the results were just as good as with regular milk, so this dish can easily be made without dairy.

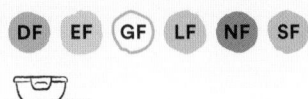

(DF) (EF) (GF) (LF) (NF) (SF)

Packed with restorative spices and low-FODMAP vegetables, this curry is a winner on all fronts: it's quick and easy to make, healthy and tasty. Serve it with white or brown rice, or quinoa, for a filling, nutritious meal.

Quick vegetable curry

Prep time: 5 minutes
Cook time: 20 minutes
Serves: 4

2 teaspoons garlic-infused
  olive oil
15 g (½ oz) crushed ginger
100 g (3½ oz) carrot, peeled and
  cut into 1–2 cm (½–¾ in) dice
½ teaspoon ground coriander
1 teaspoon ground cumin
½ teaspoon ground turmeric
½ teaspoon ground cinnamon
½ teaspoon chilli flakes
1 teaspoon salt
½ teaspoon black pepper
2 teaspoons tomato paste
  (concentrated purée)
160 ml (5¼ fl oz) coconut cream
300 ml (10½ fl oz) water or
  Low-FODMAP chicken stock
  (page 217)
1 low-FODMAP chicken stock
  cube (omit if using chicken
  stock)
100 g (3½ oz) potato, peeled
  and cut into 1–2 cm (½–¾ in)
  dice
1 fresh tomato, cut into 2 cm
  (¾ in) dice
130 g (4¾ oz) broccoli florets
½ cup (25 g) baby spinach

Heat the garlic oil in a large saucepan for 1–2 minutes over medium–high heat, then add the ginger and sauté for 2 minutes, or until fragrant.

Add the carrot and cook for 2–3 minutes, then add the spices, salt and pepper and cook for a further 1–2 minutes, or until fragrant. Add the tomato paste, coconut cream, water and stock cube (or chicken stock) and bring to the boil. Reduce the heat to medium and add the potato. Simmer for 10 minutes, or until the carrot and potato have softened, then add the tomato and broccoli. Simmer for another 10 minutes, then add the spinach and turn off the heat. Stir until the spinach is wilted.

Serve straight away over a grain of your choice or store in the fridge for up to 3–4 days, or in portions in the freezer for up to 3 months.

For the best results, allow to thaw overnight in the fridge, then heat in the microwave for 2–3 minutes, stirring halfway through, until evenly heated. You can also reheat it from frozen in the microwave for 4–6 minutes.

Miso eggplant (aubergine) is such an underrated meal. Soft, rich eggplant is coated in a sweet and salty, umami-rich sauce – it is mouthwateringly good! I love it paired with sesame rice and Asian greens for a filling meal.

Miso eggplant with sesame rice

Prep time: 10 minutes
Cook time: 20–30 minutes
Serves: 4

2 small eggplants (aubergines; see Tip)
1–2 tablespoons extra-virgin olive oil
salt and black pepper, to taste
sesame seeds, for sprinkling

Sesame rice

1 cup (250 g) white rice, rinsed and drained
2 tablespoons toasted sesame seeds
50 g (1¾ oz) spring onion (scallion), green part only, finely chopped
1 teaspoon chilli flakes
2 teaspoons sesame oil
1½ tablespoons soy sauce

Miso glaze

40 g (1½ oz) white miso paste
2 tablespoons rice-wine vinegar
25 g (1 oz) soft brown sugar

Preheat the oven to 180°C (350°F).

For the sesame rice, add the rice to a saucepan with 2 cups (500 ml) cold water. Bring to the boil over high heat, then reduce the heat to low, cover and simmer for 15–20 minutes, or until all the water has evaporated and the rice is cooked through, then drain. If you prefer, you can use a rice cooker.

While the rice is cooking, combine all the miso glaze ingredients in a bowl with 2 tablespoons water and mix until combined.

Cut the eggplants in half lengthways and score the flesh in a grid pattern. Drizzle with the oil and season with salt and pepper.

Place on a baking tray and roast for 15 minutes, then remove from the oven and spoon the miso glaze generously onto the scored side of the eggplants. Increase the oven temperature to 200°C (400°F) and cook the eggplant with the miso glaze for another 8–10 minutes. Remove from the oven and sprinkle with some sesame seeds.

Once the rice is cooked, add all the other ingredients and mix gently to combine. Serve with the eggplant.

Tip: If the eggplants are large, you may need to cut them a bit smaller, as eggplant is only low FODMAP at 75 g (2¾ oz) per serve.

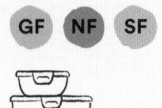

These fritters are not only perfect for lunch, but they also make a nutritious breakfast. Top with a poached egg or two and you have a perfectly balanced meal.

Sweet potato and zucchini fritters with rocket parmesan salad

Prep time: 15 minutes
Cook time: 25 minutes
Serves: 5

425 g (15 oz) zucchini
  (courgette), grated
200 g (7 oz) sweet potato, grated
3 eggs
130 g (4¾ oz) plain (all-purpose)
  flour of your choice
1 tablespoon dried chives
½ teaspoon ground cumin
½ teaspoon ground coriander
½ teaspoon ground turmeric
½ teaspoon baking powder
½ teaspoon salt, plus extra for
  the zucchini
½ teaspoon black pepper
¼ cup (60 ml) extra-virgin
  olive oil

Salad
2¾ cups (100 g) rocket (arugula)
30 g (1 oz) shaved parmesan
  cheese
30–60 ml (1–2 fl oz) The best
  balsamic dressing (page 209)

Place the zucchini in a bowl and sprinkle generously with the extra salt. Leave to sit for 10–15 minutes until the water starts to come out. This is an important step to prevent soggy fritters.

Strain the zucchini through pieces of muslin (cheesecloth), or through clean disposable cloth, pressing against a sieve to remove excess water.

In a bowl, combine the zucchini with all the remaining ingredients, except the oil, and mix until well combined.

Heat the oil in a frying pan and cook a small amount of the mixture. Taste it and adjust the seasoning in the rest of the mixture, if necessary.

Add ¼ cup portions of the mixture to the pan and cook over medium–high heat for 2–3 minutes on each side or until golden brown.

Finally, I like to finish these off in the oven for another 5–8 minutes at 180°C (350°F), turning halfway through. This step is not necessary, but I find it dries out some of the excess moisture in the fritters, which makes them keep a little longer.

Store in the fridge for 3–4 days or freeze for 3 months. If freezing, I like to add some baking paper between the fritters so they don't freeze in one clump. It also allows you to easily defrost just one or two at a time.

To reheat, simply thaw in the fridge overnight or defrost in the microwave at 30-second intervals. You can reheat the defrosted fritters in an air fryer for 2–3 minutes or in a frying pan over medium–high heat, or just pop them in the toaster!

To serve, mix the salad ingredients together in a bowl and serve alongside the fritters.

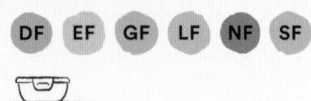

DF **EF** **GF** **LF** **NF** **SF**

Slow-cooked vegetables in a tomato sauce really is comfort food at its finest. The best part is this dish is so simple to make and comes together in one pot. This makes for a great side dish, or you can add some crumbled feta cheese, olives and pine nuts for a more satisfying standalone meal – oh, and don't forget the crusty bread!

One-pot ratatouille

Prep time: 10 minutes
Cook time: 30 minutes
Serves: 4

2 tablespoons garlic-infused
   olive oil
1 tablespoon extra-virgin olive oil
400 g (14 oz) eggplant
   (aubergine), cut into 5 cm
   (2 in) dice
330 g (11¾ oz) zucchini
   (courgette), cut into 1 cm
   (½ in) thick rounds
270 g (9½ oz) green capsicum
   (pepper), cut into 5 cm
   (2 in) dice
270 g (9½ oz) red capsicum
   (pepper), cut into 5 cm
   (2 in) dice
830 g (1 lb 13 oz) tinned diced
   tomato
2 teaspoons salt
½ teaspoon black pepper
1 tablespoon dried chives
1 teaspoon dried oregano
1 teaspoon dried basil
1 teaspoon sweet paprika
fresh basil leaves, to serve
   (optional)
toasted pine nuts, to serve
gluten-free bread, chargrilled,
   to serve

Heat the oils in a large saucepan over high heat for 1–2 minutes, then add the vegetables. Sauté for 5 minutes, then add the tinned tomato with all the remaining ingredients. Bring to the boil, then reduce the heat to medium–low and simmer for 20–30 minutes, or until the vegetables are cooked though.

Garnish with basil, if desired, scatter with pine nuts and serve with chargrilled bread – it's great with the ratatouille heaped on top or used to mop up the sauce.

Served as a side or a standalone meal, this creamy potato bake is truly one to bookmark for when you need a cosy, comforting dinner. I would describe this as a healthier cousin to potato gratin, as it has both broccoli and spinach but no bacon (although this is an addition I would support!).

Creamy broccoli and potato cheesy bake

Prep time: 5 minutes
Cook time: 1 hour
Serves: 4–6

500 g (1 lb 2 oz) potato, peeled and cut into 2 cm (¾ in) dice
2 cups (120 g) broccoli florets
1½ cups (50 g) baby spinach

Cheese sauce
70 ml (2¼ fl oz) canola oil or other neutral-flavoured oil
2 teaspoons extra-virgin olive oil, plus extra for greasing
40 g (1½ oz) cornflour (cornstarch)
4 cups (1 litre) milk of your choice
1½ teaspoons dijon mustard
60 g (2¼ oz) grated cheddar cheese, plus extra for topping
20 g (¾ oz) grated parmesan cheese, plus 3 tablespoons extra for topping
2 teaspoons salt
½ teaspoon black pepper

Preheat the oven to 180°C (350°F).

Grease a 33 × 23 cm (13 × 9 in) roasting tin or baking dish with oil, then evenly spread out the potato, broccoli and spinach in the base.

To make the cheese sauce, heat the oils in a large saucepan over high heat for 1–2 minutes. Add the cornflour and whisk continuously for another 1–2 minutes, taking care to scrape down the side of the pan to prevent any burning or sticking.

Slowly add the milk and continue to whisk until the sauce comes to the boil and thickens. It may take some time, but it will thicken up. Make sure to stir continuously to prevent the sauce from catching on the bottom of the pan.

Once the sauce is boiling and has thickened, remove from the heat and add the remaining ingredients. Whisk until the cheeses have melted.

Carefully pour the cheese sauce into the tin over the potato, broccoli and spinach. Cover with aluminium foil and bake for 40–50 minutes, or until a knife easily pierces a piece of potato.

Remove the foil and sprinkle the extra cheeses on top, then return to the oven and cook for another 5–10 minutes, or until the cheese has melted and browned.

Allow to cool for 10–15 minutes before serving.

Cooking the grains in stock in this recipe creates such a great depth of flavour that is often lacking in vegetable dishes. Once you try it, you won't be able to go back to cooking grains in plain water. Serve this as a side dish or add some protein, such as chicken or tofu, to make it a main meal.

Roasted vegetable grain salad with creamy pesto dressing

Prep time: 5 minutes
Cook time: 25 minutes
Serves: 3–4

½ cup (100 g) quinoa or grain of your choice (see Tips)

1¼ cups (310 ml) Low-FODMAP chicken stock (page 217) or vegetable stock

170 g (6 oz) kabocha (Japanese) pumpkin (squash), cut into 1–2 cm (½–¾ in) dice

200 g (7 oz) zucchini (courgette), cut into 1–2 cm (½–¾ in) dice

100 g (3½ oz) red capsicum (pepper), cut into 1–2 cm (½–¾ in) dice

100 g (3½ oz) carrot, cut into 1–2 cm (½–¾ in) dice

2 tablespoons extra-virgin olive oil

½ teaspoon salt

¼ teaspoon black pepper

½ teaspoon dried basil

30 g (1 oz) pitted kalamata (black) olives, sliced

40 g (1½ oz) feta cheese (optional)

30 g (1 oz) flaked toasted almonds (optional) or substitute for seeds to keep it nut free

Preheat the oven to 180°C (350°F).

Wash the quinoa in a sieve under cold running water, then drain. Add the quinoa to a saucepan with the stock. Bring to the boil over high heat, then reduce the heat to low, cover and simmer for 15–20 minutes, or until the stock is absorbed and the quinoa is cooked. Leave to cool slightly.

While the quinoa is cooking, add all the chopped vegetables to a roasting tin and coat with the oil, salt, pepper and basil. Roast for 20–25 minutes, or until the vegetables are soft and cooked through. Remove and leave to cool slightly.

While the quinoa and vegetables are cooling, make the creamy pesto dressing. Simply add all the ingredients to a small bowl and mix well.

Assemble the salad by combining the quinoa, vegetables and olives, along with the feta and almonds, if using.

Serve the salad with the dressing on the side – perfection!

Tips: You can use any grain you like with this salad. Try farro (if tolerated), or you could use buckwheat, brown rice or a mixture of grains.

To save time, you can also use ready-made microwave grain packets, such as a quinoa and brown rice blend. There are heaps of these available in supermarkets these days, so feel free to substitute.

I use Basil pesto (page 206) in this recipe, but if you are dairy free or nut free, substitute with the Kale pesto (page 206).

Creamy pesto dressing
¼ cup (70 g) Greek yoghurt
   or yoghurt of your choice
30 g (1 oz) Whole-egg
   mayonnaise (page 202) or
   store-bought mayo
½ teaspoon dijon mustard
3 teaspoons Basil pesto
   (page 206; see Tips)

DF EF GF LF NF SF

Couscous is made from wheat and is high in fructans. Quinoa is similar in appearance and texture but is also gluten free – and a great source of protein, too!

Quinoa 'couscous' salad

Prep time: 10 minutes
Cook time: 20 minutes
Serves: 4–6

1 cup (200 g) quinoa
1 continental cucumber
2 tomatoes
1 cup (20 g) flat-leaf (Italian) parsley leaves, finely chopped
½ cup (25 g) mint leaves, finely chopped

Dressing
½ cup (125 ml) extra-virgin olive oil
1½ tablespoons lemon juice
½ teaspoon salt
¼ teaspoon black pepper
¼ teaspoon ground cumin

Put the quinoa in a sieve and wash thoroughly under cold running water. Drain, then add it to a saucepan with 2¼ cups (560 ml) water and bring to the boil over high heat. Once boiling, reduce the heat to low, cover and simmer for 15–20 minutes, or until the quinoa is cooked and the water has evaporated. Allow to cool completely.

While the quinoa is cooling, cut the cucumber in half lengthways and scrape out the seeds with a teaspoon. Finely dice into 5 mm (¼ in) pieces. Do the same with the tomato, removing the seeds to avoid the couscous becoming soggy or wet. Finely dice into 5 mm (¼ in) pieces.

Add the cucumber and tomato to the chopped parsley and mint, then add the cooled quinoa and toss to combine. Finally, add the dressing ingredients and toss to combine. Taste and adjust the seasoning if needed.

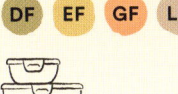

DF EF GF LF NF SF

Traditional falafels are made with chickpeas or beans and are too high in FODMAPs, so I created this recipe, which is not only low FODMAP but possibly even better than the original! This is my sister's favourite dish, and when she heard I was writing a cookbook, her first question was, 'Will the falafels be in it?' She loves them because these falafels aren't dry like traditional chickpea ones can be. By using potato instead of legumes, these falafels are soft and fluffy, yet still have the authentic flavour of the ones we know and love.

I have two different serving options to show just how versatile these are. You can shape them into balls or patties and even fry them in a little oil if you want a crunchier, more authentic exterior. You can also use them in wraps, add them to your favourite salad or even serve as an appetiser with Tzatziki (pages 146–7).

Faux-lafels

Prep time: 5 minutes
Cook time: 40 minutes
Serves: 6

700 g (1 lb 9 oz) potatoes, peeled and cut into 2 cm (¾ in) dice
50 g (1¾ oz) pepitas (pumpkin seeds)
3 teaspoons ground cumin
1 teaspoon ground turmeric
1 teaspoon sweet paprika
1 tablespoon dried chives
3 tablespoons dried parsley
1 tablespoon garlic-infused olive oil
1 tablespoon extra-virgin olive oil
½ teaspoon salt
½ teaspoon black pepper

Put the potato in a stockpot and add enough cold salted water to cover the potato by 2 cm (¾ in). Bring to the boil over high heat, then reduce the heat to medium and boil for 15–20 minutes, or until the potato can be easily pierced with a fork. Drain and allow to cool slightly before mashing.

Blitz the pepitas in a blender until finely crushed, then add to the mashed potato along with all the other ingredients and mix well to combine.

Preheat the oven to 200°C (400°F).

While the oven is heating, divide the mixture into six balls and shape into patties (see Tips). Place on a baking tray lined with baking paper and bake for 5–10 minutes on each side until golden brown.

The falafels can be frozen for up to 4 months. Just add some baking paper between each one to prevent them from freezing in one lump. Leave to thaw in the fridge overnight, or microwave for 2–3 minutes.

Tips: You can shape these into balls if you prefer a more authentic shape.

Shallow-fry the patties instead of cooking in the oven for a crispy, golden finish.

This recipe uses the Faux-lafels on page 125. Simply grill or roast vegetables of your choice (I like to use eggplant/aubergine and pumpkin/squash) in the oven or on your barbecue, fry some haloumi cheese and your life will never be the same again! This is also great with Kale pesto (page 206).

Faux-lafel burger with roasted vegetables and grilled haloumi

Prep time: 10 minutes
Cook time: 20 minutes
Serves: 6

1 eggplant (aubergine), cut into
   1 cm (½ in) thick rounds
150 g (5½ oz) kabocha
   (Japanese) pumpkin (squash),
   cut into 1 cm (½ in) thick slices
⅓–½ cup (80–120 ml)
   extra-virgin olive oil
300 g (10½ oz) haloumi cheese,
   cut into 5 mm (¼ in) thick
   slices
⅓ cup (approx. 60 g) Kale pesto
   (page 206; optional)
6 burger buns of your choice
1 cup (35 g) rocket (arugula)
6 Faux-lafel patties, cooked
   (page 125)
⅓ cup Whole-egg mayonnaise
   (page 202)
salt and black pepper, to taste

Preheat the oven to 180°C (350°F) or the barbecue to high heat.

Place the eggplant and pumpkin on baking trays and drizzle half of the oil on top. Season with salt and pepper and roast for 15–20 minutes, or until cooked through. If you're using the barbecue, toss the vegetables in the oil, salt and pepper in a large bowl and grill for 3–4 minutes on each side.

Heat the remaining oil in a frying pan over high heat, then reduce the heat to medium–low and add the haloumi slices. Fry for 1–2 minutes on each side or until golden brown. The haloumi will soften as it cooks, so be careful when removing it. Serve the haloumi as hot as possible, as it will harden as it cools and lose that delicious soft, gooey texture.

Spread some kale pesto (if using) on the bottom half of the burger buns, then top with a faux-lafel patty, some roasted pumpkin and eggplant, the freshly grilled haloumi and some rocket. Spread some mayo on the top half of the bun and sandwich together.

Tip: You can make the faux-lafel patties ahead of time and also roast the vegetables the day before for an even quicker meal.

DF EF GF LF NF SF

Flavoursome, herby rice stuffed generously into ripe tomatoes and roasted in the oven with potatoes. It tastes as good as it sounds! This is a classic Mediterranean dish that can also be made with zucchini (courgette) or eggplants (aubergine). Just be sure to keep an eye on portion sizes (see page 14) to keep it low FODMAP.

Gemista rice and herb-stuffed tomatoes with potato wedges

Prep time: 20 minutes
Cook time: 1 hour
Serves: 4–6

8 large ripe tomatoes
20 g (¾ oz) spring onion
   (scallion), green top only,
   finely chopped
½ tablespoon garlic-infused
   olive oil
20 g (¾ oz) flat-leaf (Italian)
   parsley, finely chopped
1 ½ teaspoons finely chopped
   mint
1 teaspoon finely chopped dill
½ tablespoon dried basil
½ tablespoon dried oregano
1½ teaspoons salt, plus extra
   for sprinkling
½ teaspoon black pepper
1½ tablespoons extra-virgin olive
   oil, plus extra for drizzling
100 g (3½ oz) medium-grain
   white rice, washed and drained
½ cup (125 g) tinned tomatoes
600 g (1 lb 5 oz) potato, peeled
   and cut into wedges

Slice 1 cm (½ in) off the tops of the tomatoes and set the tops aside. Scoop out the tomato flesh into a bowl – this will be added to the stuffing mix. Be careful not to pierce the side of the tomatoes; just remove the liquid and seeds to make a nice cavity for the stuffing.

Using a hand-held or high-speed blender, purée the tomato flesh until as smooth as possible.

To make the stuffing, combine all the ingredients, except the potato, in a bowl with the tomato flesh and mix well. Stuff the tomatoes, filling them to just below the top, as the rice will expand as it cooks.

Preheat the oven to 180°C (350°F).

Toss the potato wedges in a bowl with some oil. If there is any leftover stuffing, mix this in with the potatoes.

Place the stuffed tomatoes in a deep roasting tin and arrange the potato wedges around the tomatoes to help keep them upright as they cook.

Add the tops of the tomatoes back onto the stuffed tomatoes like little hats, drizzle the tomatoes with some olive oil and sprinkle with a little extra salt. Add ¼ cup (60 ml) water to the baking dish – just pour it in one corner and let it spread so as not to wash the seasoning off the potatoes.

Cook for 1 hour, or until the rice is cooked and the potatoes are golden brown.

These arancini are perfect as an appetiser or even as a snack. I like to bake them, but you can fry them in oil if you prefer. Baking makes them a little less naughty but, don't worry, they still have that irresistible crunchy shell. Arancini are traditionally served with Napoli sauce (page 214), but I also like to dip them in Whole-egg mayonnaise (page 202) or Cheat's aioli (page 203).

Baked arancini

Prep time: 15 minutes
Cook time: 30 minutes
Makes: 24

3–4 cups (750 ml–1 litre)
    Low-FODMAP chicken stock
    (page 217)
2 tablespoons extra-virgin
    olive oil
1 cup (220 g) arborio rice or
    other medium-grain white rice,
    washed and drained
2 teaspoons garlic-infused
    olive oil
½ teaspoon salt
1 teaspoon dried basil
½ teaspoon black pepper
½ cup (25 g) grated cheese
    of your choice, plus extra
    for stuffing
2 eggs
1½ cups (150 g) Breadcrumbs
    (page 218) or store-bought
    breadcrumbs

Heat the chicken stock in a large saucepan over medium heat until hot, then reduce the heat to low and keep on a gentle simmer.

Heat the oil in another saucepan over medium–high heat and add the rice. Cook for 1–2 minutes to toast the grains and warm them up.

Add the garlic oil, salt, basil and pepper, followed by about ½ cup (125 ml) of the chicken stock. Stir until the stock has been almost completely absorbed, then add another ½ cup (125 ml) of stock. Continue this process until the rice is al dente. It is important to continuously stir, as this will make a creamy risotto by releasing the starches in the rice.

Once the rice is cooked, mix in the cheese until melted, then spread the risotto on a baking tray or large plate and allow to cool. Once cooled, place in the fridge for 30 minutes to chill.

By now, the rice should be sticky. Using well-oiled hands, take tablespoons of the risotto and flatten onto the palm of your hand. Next, add some grated cheese to the middle – about ½–1 teaspoon. Bring the edges together into the centre so that the cheese is in the middle and roll into balls (see Tip). Place on a baking tray lined with baking paper and refrigerate for another 20 minutes, or even overnight.

Preheat the oven to 200°C (400°F).

Crack the eggs into a shallow bowl and beat together. Place the breadcrumbs in another bowl. Remove the rice balls from the fridge and dip first into the egg, then into the breadcrumbs, working one at a time. Once the balls have been crumbed, place back on the baking tray and bake for 20–30 minutes, flipping halfway through, until golden brown.

Allow to cool slightly before serving.

Tip: You can use cheese cut into 1 cm (½ in) cubes if you prefer. I prefer to use grated cheese, as I find it faster and easier (less cutting).

These meals are great for the whole family, and even the little ones will happily chow down, whether they're on a low-FODMAP diet or not! From noodles to meatballs to fish and chips, these recipes are sure to become family favourites in no time.

Family

Faves

Anyone who's been to IKEA will know Swedish meatballs – and how moreish they are! So, here is a version of this food-hall favourite that you can trust. These meatballs have the perfect balance of spice and richness from the sauce. I love the nutmeg and allspice in this recipe and the unique flavour the spices bring.

Swedish meatballs with mashed potato

Prep time: 15 minutes
Cook time: 30 minutes
Serves: 4

Meatballs
400 g (14 oz) minced (ground) beef
40 g (1½ oz) Breadcrumbs (page 218) or store bought
1½ tablespoons milk of your choice
1 egg
2 teaspoons garlic-infused olive oil
1 teaspoon dried chives
½ teaspoon salt
⅛ teaspoon black pepper
⅛ teaspoon ground nutmeg
⅛ teaspoon ground allspice
2–3 tablespoons extra-virgin olive oil

Mashed potato
700 g (1 lb 9 oz) potatoes, peeled and cut into 3 cm (1¼ in) dice
1 tablespoon butter or dairy-free alternative
¼ cup (60 ml) milk of your choice
salt, to taste

Add all the ingredients for the meatballs, except the oil, to a large bowl or stand mixer fitted with the paddle attachment and mix together until well combined. Roll into approximately twelve 40 g (1½ oz) balls.

Place the potato for the mash in a large stockpot and cover with cold salted water. Bring to the boil over high heat. Once boiling, reduce the heat to a medium–high and simmer until the potato is tender enough to break when pressed on the side of the pot with a fork, about 15–20 minutes. Drain, then mash the potato and mix in the butter, milk and salt.

While the potatoes are cooking, heat the oil for the meatballs in a frying pan over medium heat and brown the meatballs on all sides. Remove from the pan and set aside.

To make the sauce, melt the butter and oil in the same pan, then add the cornflour and stir for 1–2 minutes. Add the water and stock cubes (or beef stock), and the milk, and bring to the boil.

Return the meatballs to the pan and simmer in the sauce for 10–12 minutes, or until cooked through. Season with salt and pepper to taste.

Serve the meatballs on top of or alongside the mashed potato with a good helping of the sauce.

Sauce

½ tablespoon butter or
   dairy-free alternative

½ tablespoon extra-virgin
   olive oil

1 tablespoon cornflour
   (cornstarch)

300 ml (10½ fl oz) water or
   Low-FODMAP beef stock
   (page 215)

2 low-FODMAP beef stock cubes
   (omit if using beef stock)

¼ cup (60 ml) milk of your
   choice

salt and black pepper, to taste

These sticky sesame chicken meatballs are easy and quick to make. Here, I use them to make banh mi–style rolls, but they can also be served with rice and vegetables, with noodles or as an appetiser. There is no real recipe to make these into banh mi, so I have simply listed the ingredients needed. All you need to do is assemble and use as much or as little filling as you like.

Banh mi with sticky sesame chicken meatballs

Prep time: 15 minutes
Cook time: 25 minutes
Makes: 24 meatballs

Chicken meatballs
500 g (1 lb 2 oz) minced
   (ground) chicken
½ cup (30 g) Breadcrumbs
   (page 218) or store-bought
   gluten-free breadcrumbs
1 tablespoon sesame seeds
½ teaspoon salt
¼ teaspoon black pepper
¼ teaspoon chilli flakes
2 tablespoons garlic-infused
   olive oil
1–2 tablespoons extra-virgin
   olive oil

Sauce
½ cup (125 ml) soy sauce
½ cup (125 ml) rice-wine vinegar
1½ teaspoons sesame oil
90 ml (3 fl oz) pure maple syrup

To serve
gluten-free bread rolls
   of your choice
Whole-egg mayonnaise
   (page 202)
grated carrot
sliced cucumber
fresh coriander (cilantro)
sliced radish (optional)

To make the meatballs, combine all the ingredients, except the extra-virgin olive oil, in a bowl and mix by hand, or use a stand mixer fitted with the paddle attachment on medium–low speed. Roll into 1 tablespoon balls (about 30 g/1 oz each). I make these small, but you can make them any size you want.

Combine all the sauce ingredients in a bowl and set aside.

Heat the extra-virgin olive oil in a frying pan over high heat, then reduce the heat to medium–high heat and brown the meatballs on all sides for 3–4 minutes, or until golden on the outside (see Tip). Add the sauce, reduce the heat to medium–low, cover and simmer for 15–20 minutes, or until the sauce has thickened and the meatballs are cooked through. Leave to cool.

Cut the bread rolls in half and spread some mayonnaise on one side, then fill with the carrot, cucumber, coriander, radish, meatballs and a drizzle of the sticky sauce.

The meatballs will keep in the fridge for up to 3–4 days or in the freezer for up to 3 months.

For the best results, allow to thaw overnight in the fridge, then heat in the microwave for 2–3 minutes. You can also reheat the meatballs from frozen in the microwave for 4–6 minutes.

Tip: You can also cook these meatballs in the oven. Just cook them in a baking dish at 220°C (425°F) for 7–10 minutes, then add the sauce and cover with aluminium foil (or it will splatter) and cook for another 10 minutes.

I am a huge lover of noodles, and this dish is so simple I find myself making it on repeat when I have a craving for a quick noodle dish. It's loaded with vegetables and comes together in a flash. It also doubles as a great side dish. You can adjust the amount of garam masala depending on how much spice you like.

Easy Singapore-style noodles

Prep time: 5 minutes
Cook time: 15 minutes
Serves: 4

200 g (7 oz) rice vermicelli
    noodles
1 tablespoon sesame oil
1 tablespoon garlic-infused
    olive oil
3 teaspoons minced or crushed
    ginger
280 g (10 oz) carrot, sliced into
    5 mm (¼ in) half-moons
270 g (9½ oz) red capsicum
    (pepper), cut into 5 mm (¼ in)
    thick slices
270 g (9½ oz) green capsicum
    (pepper), cut into 5 mm (¼ in)
    thick slices
1–2 teaspoons garam masala
90 ml (3 fl oz) soy sauce
5 eggs
2 tablespoons extra-virgin
    olive oil
salt and black pepper, to taste

Cook the noodles according to the packet instructions, then drain and rinse under cold running water.

Heat the sesame and garlic oils in a wok or large frying pan over high heat. Add the ginger and sauté for 1–2 minutes, or until fragrant. Add the carrot and cook for 3–4 minutes, or until it's beginning to soften. Add the red and green capsicum, along with the garam masala and soy sauce, then cook for another 4 minutes or until the vegetables are soft.

Add the noodles and toss quickly to coat in the sauce, then season with salt and pepper. Remove from the pan.

Add the oil to the same pan and crack in the eggs. Season with salt and pepper, then scramble with a spatula until just cooked through. Add the scrambled eggs to the noodles and toss to combine.

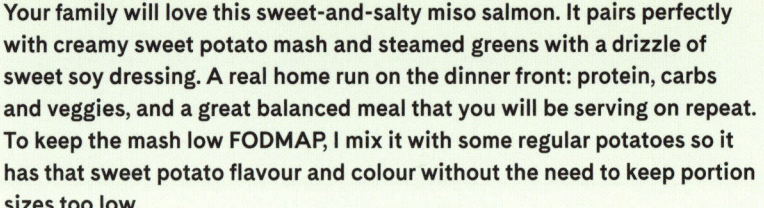

Your family will love this sweet-and-salty miso salmon. It pairs perfectly with creamy sweet potato mash and steamed greens with a drizzle of sweet soy dressing. A real home run on the dinner front: protein, carbs and veggies, and a great balanced meal that you will be serving on repeat. To keep the mash low FODMAP, I mix it with some regular potatoes so it has that sweet potato flavour and colour without the need to keep portion sizes too low.

Miso salmon with sweet potato mash, greens and soy dressing

Prep time: 5 minutes
Cook time: 35 minutes
Serves: 4

400 g (14 oz) skinless salmon
   fillets
sesame seeds, to garnish
   (optional)
3⅓ cups (200 g) broccoli florets
200 g (7 oz) green beans

Miso glaze
40 g (1½ oz) white miso paste
2 tablespoons rice-wine vinegar
25 g (1 oz) soft brown sugar

Sweet potato mash
500 g (1 lb 2 oz) russet or other
   floury potato, peeled and cut
   into 3 cm (1¼ in) dice
200 g (7 oz) sweet potato,
   peeled and cut into 3 cm
   (1¼ in) dice
1 tablespoon butter or dairy-free
   alternative
¼ cup (60 ml) milk of your choice
salt and black pepper, to taste

Soy dressing
2 tablespoons soy sauce
2 teaspoons sesame oil
1 tablespoon garlic-infused
   olive oil
1 tablespoon soft brown sugar

Preheat the oven to 200°C (400°F).

Make the miso glaze by mixing all the ingredients in a small bowl with 2 tablespoons water until well combined. Set aside.

For the mash, put the diced potato and sweet potato in a large saucepan and cover with cold water. Season generously with salt, then bring to the boil over high heat. Once boiling, reduce the heat slightly so it is not boiling too rapidly. Cook for 15–20 minutes until the potatoes are cooked and break apart when gently crushed against the side of the pot. Drain and mash until smooth. Add the butter and milk and season with salt and pepper to taste.

While the potatoes are cooking, line a baking tray with baking paper and place the salmon fillets on the tray. Coat the salmon in half the miso glaze and bake for 15–20 minutes, or until cooked to your liking. Once the salmon is cooked, spread the remaining miso glaze on top and sprinkle with sesame seeds, if using.

I like to steam the greens in the microwave by putting them in a microwave-safe container with 1–2 tablespoons cold water, covering and cooking for 4 minutes, but you can also boil or steam them on the stovetop if you prefer.

For the soy dressing, simply mix all the ingredients together and drizzle over the greens once cooked.

Serve the salmon with the mash and greens on the side.

Making your own breadcrumbs (page 218) truly raises the classic chicken schnitzel to new heights. I know this might be controversial, but I don't worry about the flour layer when making schnitzel – I just use egg wash and breadcrumbs. It's one less step, which means less time and less cleaning! This is perfect served with a simple salad or vegetables.

Chicken schnitzel with homemade breadcrumbs

Prep time: 15 minutes
Cook time: 20 minutes
Serves: 4

2 × 200 g (7 oz) skinless
   chicken breasts
3 eggs
2–3 cups (120–180 g)
   Breadcrumbs (page 218;
   see Tips) or store bought
canola oil or other neutral-
   flavoured oil, for shallow-frying
salt, to taste

Slice each chicken breast fillet in half to make four fillets. Cover the fillets in plastic wrap or place in a freezer bag and use a meat mallet or rolling pin to bash them to an even thickness, about 5 mm–1 cm (¼–½ in).

Whisk the eggs in a flat, wide bowl. To another flat, wide bowl add the breadcrumbs.

Dip each chicken fillet first into the egg, then into the breadcrumbs. Coat the chicken on all sides, pressing down firmly to make sure the crumbs stick well. Transfer the crumbed chicken to a clean plate and continue until all the chicken is crumbed.

Add enough oil to a frying pan so it is about 1–2 cm (½–¾ in) deep. We are shallow-frying here, so you don't need too much, and you can always add more as you go. Place the pan over high heat for 3–4 minutes to get the oil nice and hot, then reduce the heat to medium–high. Test the oil by dropping in a pinch of breadcrumbs – they should immediately start gently frying.

Carefully add the chicken, one or two fillets at a time, depending on how big your frying pan is. They should be frying gently and not too aggressively, so adjust the temperature as needed. Fry for 2–3 minutes on each side, then transfer to a plate lined with paper towel to absorb the excess oil. Season generously with salt and serve.

Tips: Feel free to use store-bought breadcrumbs, but I recommend adding the herbs and seasonings I use in the Breadcrumbs recipe (page 218).

To turn this into a parma, simply add some Napoli sauce (page 214) to the cooked schnitzels along with some mozzarella cheese, then grill (broil) in the oven for 5 minutes or until the cheese has melted (you can also add some ham before the cheese as well).

Cut the chicken into smaller pieces and turn this into chicken nuggets, if you like.

This recipe for beer-battered fish is always a winner, and it's surprisingly easy! I like to use haddock, but you can also use cod, flake or really any type of white, fleshy fish. I have made this with gluten-free beer before, too, and it is fantastic. This is equally delicious served with Napoli sauce (page 214).

Beer-battered fish and chips with tartare sauce

Prep time: 15 minutes
Cook time: 30 minutes
Serves: 6–8

500 g (1 lb 2 oz) skinless
   haddock fillets
canola oil or other neutral-
   flavoured oil, for deep-frying
600 g (1 lb 5 oz) potatoes,
   peeled and cut into chips
   1 cm (½ in) thick (see Tip)

Tartare sauce
2 teaspoons capers, finely
   chopped
1½ teaspoons fresh dill, finely
   chopped
½ cup (120 g) Whole-egg
   mayonnaise (page 202) or
   store-bought mayo
1 teaspoon dijon mustard
2 teaspoons lemon juice

Batter
1 cup (150 g) plain (all-purpose)
   flour
½ cup (75 g) self-raising flour
½ teaspoon baking powder
½ teaspoon salt
¼ teaspoon black pepper
1–1¾ cups (435 ml) beer of your
   choice

Make the tartare sauce by combining all the ingredients in a small bowl. Store in an airtight container in the fridge for 3–4 days.

Cut the fish in half lengthways, then cut into smaller pieces (approx. 10–12 cm/4–4½ in) for frying.

To make the batter, combine all the dry ingredients in a bowl and slowly add the beer, whisking until a smooth batter forms. The batter should be thick but pourable, similar to pancake batter. If you lift up the whisk and draw a figure of 8, it should sit on the surface of the batter briefly before disappearing.

Heat enough canola oil for deep-frying in a large saucepan over high heat. Allow the oil to get nice and hot, about 2–3 minutes, then drop in a small amount of batter to test the temperature. The oil is ready when the batter immediately starts frying and floats to the surface. Working in batches, dip the fish pieces into the batter and gently add to the oil.

Working in batches, fry the fish until golden brown on all sides, about 5–8 minutes. You may need to turn down the heat – the fish should be frying gently, not too aggressively. Once golden brown, transfer the fish to a plate lined with paper towel to drain the excess oil. Repeat until all the fish is cooked.

Use the same oil to fry the potato to make chips (fries). Add the potato to the oil, working in batches if necessary, and fry until nicely browned and cooked through. Drain on some paper towel before seasoning with salt and serving with the fish and tartare sauce.

Tip: If you're feeling extra adventurous, try your hand at some homemade potato cakes! Simply cut potatoes into thin rounds, dip into the batter and fry for 2–3 minutes on each side until golden brown. You can also serve this with baked potatoes or air-fried potatoes.

Souvlaki has always been a taste of home for me, and this version with tender lamb backstrap is no exception. The secret to any good souvlaki is tender, marinated meat and, of course, the tzatziki. You will be surprised by how much this tzatziki recipe tastes like the original. This is all thanks to my friend garlic oil; it truly is a saviour for adding authentic flavour to dishes while keeping them low FODMAP. If you can't tolerate it, you can omit it and the tzatziki will still be delicious, just not as authentic. I have also included a recipe for yeast-free pita bread. It's not as light and fluffy as yeasted pita bread, but it is a great recipe when you need something quick and easy.

Souvlaki with tzatziki

Prep time: 10 minutes, plus marinating
Cook time: 15–20 minutes
Serves: 4

Meat
500 g (1 lb 2 oz) lamb backstrap or pork loin, cut into 3 cm (1¼ in) chunks
2 tablespoons extra-virgin olive oil, plus extra for frying
1½ teaspoons salt
1 teaspoon black pepper
1 tablespoon dried oregano
1 teaspoon smoked paprika
1 tablespoon lemon juice

Yeast-free pita bread
3¾ cups (460 g) plain (all-purpose) flour, plus extra for dusting
2 tablespoons baking powder
1½ teaspoons salt
100 ml (3½ fl oz) extra-virgin olive oil, plus 1–2 tablespoons extra for frying
1½ cups (375 ml) warm water

Add the lamb backstrap to a bowl with all the other meat ingredients, mix well, cover and marinate in the fridge for 2–4 hours.

For the pita bread, add all the dry ingredients to a bowl and mix well. Add the oil and water and mix until a dough forms. If you're using regular wheat flour, set the dough aside to rest for 20–30 minutes.

Portion the dough into four pieces and roll into balls. Dust your benchtop with flour and roll the balls into discs. I find gluten-free flour easier to work with if you roll it between sheets of baking paper, which also makes it easier to lift and transfer to the pan for cooking.

Heat some extra oil in a large frying pan over medium–high heat and, once hot, fry the pita breads for 2–3 minutes on each side until golden brown. The bread should puff up with little air pockets. Continue until all the pitas are cooked, adding more oil as needed.

For the meat, heat another frying pan with some extra oil over high heat. Remove the meat from the marinade and add to the pan, then reduce the heat to medium–high and cook for 1–2 minutes on each side until nicely browned and cooked to your liking.

To make the tzatziki, put the cucumber in a piece of muslin (cheesecloth) or clean disposable cloth, twist and squeeze out the excess liquid. Add to a bowl and mix with the other tzatziki ingredients. Taste and adjust the seasoning if necessary.

To assemble the souvlaki, simply spread some tzatziki on the pita, add some lettuce and sliced tomato and top with meat. Wrap and enjoy!

Tzatziki

1⅓ cups (250 g) grated
    cucumber
280 g (10 oz) yoghurt of your
    choice
1½ tablespoons white vinegar
1 tablespoon garlic-infused
    olive oil
1 tablespoon finely chopped
    fresh dill
½ teaspoon salt

To serve
shredded lettuce
sliced tomato

These meatballs are flavoursome and a great staple recipe to earmark, as they also make tasty appetisers. I love a meatball's versatility: add it to a crusty baguette and you have a meatball sub; add it to a pita pocket with some tzatziki and you have a makeshift souvlaki (see page 146). The possibilities are endless!

Spaghetti and meatballs

Prep time: 15 minutes
Cook time: 40 minutes
Serves: 6
Makes: approx. 20–25 meatballs

500 g (1 lb 2 oz) minced
    (ground) beef
1 cup (60 g) Breadcrumbs
    (page 218) or store bought
1 egg, lightly beaten
2 tablespoons garlic-infused
    olive oil
1 tablespoon dried oregano
1 tablespoon dried or fresh basil
2 teaspoons salt
½ teaspoon black pepper
½ teaspoon chilli flakes
    (optional)
2–3 tablespoons extra-virgin
    olive oil
1 quantity Napoli sauce
    (page 214) or 3 cups (750 g)
    store-bought alternative
400 g (14 oz) spaghetti of
    your choice

Combine all the ingredients, except the extra-virgin olive oil, Napoli sauce and spaghetti, in a bowl and mix well. Roll heaped tablespoons of the mixture into meatballs and place on a plate.

Bring a saucepan of salted water to the boil for the pasta.

While the water is coming to the boil, heat the oil in a frying pan over medium–high heat and add the meatballs. Brown on all sides for 5–10 minutes, or until golden.

Add the Napoli sauce and reduce the heat to low. Simmer for 20–30 minutes, or until the meatballs are cooked through.

Meanwhile, cook the spaghetti according to the packet instructions. Drain, adding ¼–½ cup (60–125 ml) of the pasta water to the meatballs to loosen the sauce.

You can add the spaghetti directly to the meatballs and sauce, or leave it separate and serve the meatballs on top of the pasta.

Store the meatballs in the fridge for up to 3–4 days or in portions in the freezer for up to 3 months.

For the best results, allow to thaw overnight in the fridge, then heat in the microwave for 2–3 minutes. You can also reheat them from frozen in the microwave for 4–6 minutes.

You won't believe how easy this recipe is. You quite literally throw everything into a baking tray and cook in the oven – so simple, and perfect for those busy family weeknights.

Quick penne alfredo pasta bake

Prep time: 5 minutes
Cook time: 45 minutes
Serves: 4

350 g (12 oz) penne of your
    choice
300 g (10½ oz) bacon, diced
    (see Tips)
4 cups (1 litre) milk of your choice
1 teaspoon salt
½ teaspoon black pepper
2 teaspoons dried basil
35 g (1¼ oz) grated parmesan
    (see Tips)
1 tablespoon garlic-infused
    olive oil

Preheat the oven to 200°C (400°F).

Add all the ingredients to a 33 × 23 cm (13 × 9 in) baking dish with 2 cups (500 ml) water and mix well. Cover with aluminium foil and bake for 40–45 minutes, or until the pasta is cooked through.

Tips: For extra flavour, you can pre-cook the bacon to get it nice and crispy, but it isn't necessary.

Feel free to double the amount of parmesan if you like your pasta bakes extra cheesy!

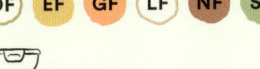 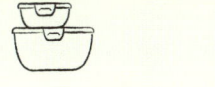

Ideal for family dinners, cosy gatherings or any time you crave a home-cooked meal, this cottage pie promises a delicious and nostalgic experience. The combination of the savoury meat filling and the smooth, crisp-topped mashed potato creates a comforting dish that's as nourishing as it is flavoursome.

Cottage pie

Prep time: 10 minutes
Cook time: 40 minutes
Serves: 4

Meat sauce

500 g (1 lb 2 oz) minced (ground) beef

75 g (2¾ oz) carrot, finely diced

1½ teaspoons dried parsley

¾ teaspoon dried rosemary

½ teaspoon dried thyme

½ teaspoon salt

½ teaspoon black pepper

30 g (1 oz) cornflour (cornstarch) or gluten-free plain (all-purpose) flour

1 tablespoon garlic-infused olive oil (optional)

40 g (1½ oz) tomato paste (concentrated purée)

1 cup (250 ml) water or Low-FODMAP beef stock (page 215)

1½ low-FODMAP beef stock cubes (omit if using beef stock)

70 g (2½ oz) zucchini (courgette), finely diced

40 g (1½ oz) frozen or tinned corn kernels

Mashed potato

800 g (1 lb 12 oz) potatoes, peeled and diced

15 g (½ oz) butter

¼ cup (60 ml) milk of your choice

salt, to taste

Place the mince in a frying pan set over medium–high heat and brown for 5–10 minutes, then add the carrot, herbs, spices and cornflour. Stir to distribute the cornflour evenly. Add the garlic oil (if using), tomato paste, water and stock cubes (or beef stock). Bring to the boil, then reduce the heat to a simmer and add the zucchini and corn. Simmer for 15–20 minutes, or until the carrot is cooked and the sauce has thickened.

While the meat sauce is cooking, add the potato to a large saucepan of cold salted water and bring to the boil over high heat. Cook for 10–15 minutes, or until a potato breaks easily when pressed against the side of the pan with a fork. Drain, then return to the pan and add the butter and milk. Mash with a potato masher until smooth, then season with salt to taste.

Preheat the oven to 180°C (350°F).

Once the meat sauce is cooked, pour it into a 23 cm (9 in) round baking dish. Allow the meat to cool slightly before topping with the mashed potato. Finish in the oven for 15–20 minutes, until the mashed potato browns slightly on top.

Enjoy straight away or store in the fridge for up to 3–4 days or in portions in the freezer for up to 3 months.

For the best results, allow to thaw overnight in the fridge, then heat in the microwave for 2–3 minutes, stirring halfway through, until evenly heated. You can also reheat it from frozen in the microwave for 4–6 minutes.

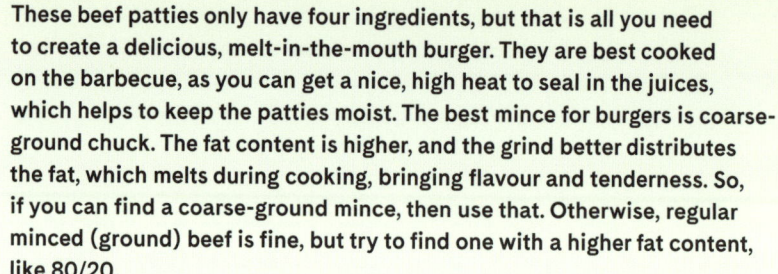

These beef patties only have four ingredients, but that is all you need to create a delicious, melt-in-the-mouth burger. They are best cooked on the barbecue, as you can get a nice, high heat to seal in the juices, which helps to keep the patties moist. The best mince for burgers is coarse-ground chuck. The fat content is higher, and the grind better distributes the fat, which melts during cooking, bringing flavour and tenderness. So, if you can find a coarse-ground mince, then use that. Otherwise, regular minced (ground) beef is fine, but try to find one with a higher fat content, like 80/20.

You can make your burger any way you please – I like it with lettuce, tomato, cheese and bacon.

Classic beef burger with eggplant and sweet potato baked chips

Prep time: 20–30 minutes
Cook time: 20 minutes
Serves: 4

2 cups (120 g) Breadcrumbs (page 218) or store-bought breadcrumbs
1 large eggplant (aubergine), cut into 2 cm (¾ in) thick chips (fries)
2 eggs, lightly beaten
2 large sweet potatoes, peeled and cut into 1 cm (½ in) thick chips
2–3 tablespoons extra-virgin olive oil, plus extra for greasing
salt and black pepper, to taste

Beef patties
500 g (1 lb 2 oz) beef chuck, coarsely ground
2 teaspoons dijon mustard
1 teaspoon salt
½ teaspoon black pepper

Preheat the oven to 200°C (400°F).

To make the beef patties, simply mix all the ingredients in a bowl and portion into 100 g (3½ oz) balls. Shape into patties.

For the eggplant chips (fries), season the breadcrumbs with salt and pepper (if using store bought). Dip the eggplant chips in the egg wash, then coat in the breadcrumbs. Arrange the crumbed eggplant on a baking tray lined with baking paper and spray with some oil. Coat the sweet potato chips with oil and season with salt and pepper. Bake for 10–15 minutes until cooked through and golden brown, turning halfway (see Tips).

Heat a barbecue chargrill to high heat and grease the plate with some oil. Place the beef patties on the hot grill and cook for 2 minutes, then flip and cook for another 2 minutes on the other side. If you are using cheese, add it after the first flip so it becomes nice and melty (see Tips). You can also cook these in a frying pan over high heat, but they won't be as flavoursome or tender, as you won't be able to achieve the higher temperature needed.

Assemble the burger with your desired toppings and a side of baked eggplant and sweet potato chips.

To serve (optional)
bread rolls of your choice
   (I like brioche for burgers)
cheese of your choice
lettuce leaves
sliced tomato
bacon
Cheat's aioli (page 203),
   Whole-egg mayonnaise
   (page 202) or store-bought
   mayo
tomato sauce (ketchup)

Tips: You can also cook the fries in an air-fryer for 5–10 minutes at 220°C (435°F). Keep an eye on them and shake regularly. I like to dip these fries in Whole-egg mayonnaise (page 202) and season with some ground paprika, or you can serve them with Maple dijon mayonnaise (page 202).

    If you have a small metal bowl, add the cheese to the burgers, then cover with a bowl so the steam melts the cheese even more. Just don't take the bowl off again with your hands! It will be hot, so use tongs.

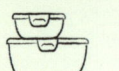

Throw this in the oven and 2–3 hours later you will have the most delicious pulled beef that is perfect for tacos, quesadillas, enchiladas, salads – the list goes on! And since avocado is low FODMAP at 60 g (2 oz), I love to serve this with some guacamole. The secret is to use lime juice for an authentic tang.

Pulled Mexican beef tacos with guacamole

Prep time: 10 minutes
Cook time: 3 hours
Serves: 4–6

Beef

½ red capsicum (pepper), quartered
1 tablespoon tomato paste (concentrated purée)
½ teaspoon ground cumin
½ teaspoon chilli flakes or chilli powder
½ teaspoon dried oregano
1 teaspoon ground coriander
½ teaspoon Tabasco sauce
1 teaspoon dried chives
1 teaspoon garlic-infused olive oil
1 kg (2 lb 4 oz) boneless beef chuck roast
1 cup (250 ml) Low-FODMAP beef stock (page 215)

Guacamole

1 ripe avocado
¼–½ small tomato, finely diced, plus extra to serve
⅛ teaspoon garlic-infused olive oil
¼ teaspoon salt
1 teaspoon spring onion (scallion), green top only, very finely diced
juice of ½ lime

Preheat the oven to 160°C (325°F).

Add the capsicum to a roasting tin.

In a bowl, mix all the other beef ingredients together, except the beef and beef stock. Rub this mixture all over the beef chuck, including underneath. Once the meat is covered in the rub (use it all), place the beef on top of the capsicum pieces in the tin. Pour the beef stock in around the meat and cover the tray with aluminium foil. Roast for 2½–3 hours.

Carefully remove the meat from the oven and take off the foil. Shred the meat right into the tin with the juices and capsicum.

When the meat is in the final stages of cooking, make the guacamole by simply mashing the avocado and mixing with all the other ingredients.

Heat the tortillas according to the packet instructions and assemble with the pulled beef, guacamole, cheese, sour cream, fresh coriander and lime wedges, if using.

The beef can be stored in the fridge for up to 3–4 days or in portions in the freezer for up to 6 days.

For the best results, allow to thaw overnight in the fridge, then heat in the microwave for 2–3 minutes. You can also reheat it from frozen in the microwave for 4–6 minutes.

To serve
tortillas of your choice
grated cheese of your choice
sour cream
fresh coriander (cilantro;
    optional)
lime wedges (optional)

A classic that us Foddies can now enjoy, too! Traditional sausage rolls use sausage meat, but I like to use minced (ground) beef as, occasionally, sausage meat includes added 'spices', which is code for onion and garlic powder – a low-FODMAP no-no. Feel free to use store-bought puff pastry for a faster and easier sausage-roll making experience.

Sausage rolls

Prep time: 30–40 minutes
Cook time: 20 minutes
Makes: 10 large or
20–25 small rolls

sesame seeds, to garnish
  (optional)
tomato sauce of choice, to serve

Filling
500 g (1 lb 2 oz) minced
  (ground) beef
40 g (1½ oz) tomato sauce
  (ketchup)
¼ teaspoon black pepper
1 teaspoon salt
1½ teaspoons dried chives
1 cup (60 g) Breadcrumbs
  (page 218)
2 eggs
1½ tablespoons garlic-infused
  olive oil
65 g (2½ oz) grated carrot
80 g (2¾ oz) grated zucchini
  (courgette)

Rough puff pastry
200 g (7 oz) butter
270 g (9½ oz) plain (all-purpose)
  flour, plus extra for dusting
  (see Tip)
130 ml (4 fl oz) cold water

For the filling, add all the ingredients, except the second egg, to the bowl of a stand mixer fitted with the paddle attachment and mix on low–medium speed until well combined. Or you can mix everything by hand – just make sure to do it thoroughly. Remove from the stand mixer bowl and wash and dry the bowl well.

To make the pastry, cut the butter into small cubes. Add all the pastry ingredients to the bowl of a stand mixer fitted with the paddle attachment and mix on medium speed until a dough forms. You can also do this by hand.

Preheat the oven to 200°C (400°F).

Divide the pastry into two to four pieces so it is more manageable to work with. Sprinkle your benchtop generously with flour and roll the pastry out into a rectangular shape about 10 cm (4 in) wide and 5 mm (¼ in) thick. Add the filling along one long edge of the dough in a sausage shape.

In a small bowl, whisk the extra egg. With your finger or a pastry brush, paint a line of egg wash along the opposite long edge of the pastry and roll up the sausage roll. Continue this process until all the dough and filling has been used. You can cut the sausage rolls into whatever size you want.

Once cut, place the sausage rolls on a baking tray lined with baking paper and brush the tops with the egg wash. Sprinkle with sesame seeds, if desired. Bake for 15–20 minutes, or until golden brown.

Enjoy straight away or store the sausage rolls in the fridge for up to 3–4 days, or in the freezer for up to 3 months.

For the best results, allow to thaw overnight in the fridge, then heat in the microwave for 2–3 minutes. You can also reheat them from frozen in the microwave for 4–6 minutes.

Tip: If you are using regular plain (all-purpose) flour instead of gluten free, you will need to rest the pastry for 20–30 minutes before rolling out, and you may not need all the water, so add it slowly.

I'm not lying when I say this is truly *the* best potato salad. I have been making it for years and it never disappoints. The secret is in making your own Whole-egg mayonnaise (page 202). It's so creamy and lip-smackingly good, you may want to keep this recipe a secret and win all the praise at family barbecues.

Best-ever potato salad

Prep time: 10 minutes
Cook time: 20 minutes
Serves: 8–10

1.4 kg (3 lb 2 oz) potato, peeled and cut into 2–3 cm (¾–1¼ in) chunks
5 eggs
100 g (3½ oz) bacon, diced
½ quantity Whole-egg mayonnaise (page 202)
1 teaspoon freshly snipped chives, plus extra to serve

Place the potato in a stockpot and cover with cold salted water by 2 cm (¾ in). Bring to the boil over high heat, then reduce the heat to medium and cook for 15–20 minutes, or until the potato can be easily pierced with a fork. Do not overcook them, as this will cause the potato to break apart and the salad to be mushy. Drain, then leave to cool in the colander.

While the potato is cooking, place the eggs in a saucepan and cover with cold water. Bring to the boil over high heat, then lower the heat to medium and boil for 10 minutes. Remove the eggs and submerge in iced water to stop the cooking process. Once cool, peel the eggs and cut each into eight to twelve pieces.

Heat a frying pan over medium heat and fry the bacon for 10–15 minutes, or until nice and crispy.

It is easiest to assemble the salad in two stages – simply add half of each ingredient to a bowl and give everything a light mix. Layer the rest of the ingredients on top and mix in. You can also gently mix everything by hand (wearing gloves) in one go.

Garnish with some extra chives and serve.

I have a massive sweet tooth and, truth be told, I prefer baking over regular cooking, so you just know these recipes are going to be winners! From brownies to shortbread, I've got you covered for quick, sweet treats that can be whipped up in no time. You'll find a couple of healthier treats in this chapter too, because a lot of the 'healthy' sweet treats out there are also high in FODMAPs because they use dates, cashews and other high-FODMAP ingredients.

The Sweet Life:

Cookies + Slices

These cookies are so easy, you can make them in one bowl by hand. You don't need any fancy equipment, and they are always a hit. They're perfect for those moments when the sweet cravings hit and you need to whip something up quickly.

Triple choc cookies

Prep time: 15 minutes
Cook time: 12 minutes
Makes: 18

160 g (5¾ oz) soft brown sugar
⅓ cup (80 ml) vegetable oil
1 egg
78 g (2¾ oz) gluten-free plain
   (all-purpose) flour
78 g (2¾ oz) gluten-free
   self-raising flour
14 g (½ oz) cocoa powder
¼ teaspoon xanthan gum
   (omit if using regular flour)
30 g (1 oz) dark chocolate chips
25 g (1 oz) milk chocolate chips
25 g (1 oz) white chocolate chips

Preheat the oven to 160°C (325°F).
   Add the sugar, oil and egg to a bowl and mix well.
Add the flours, cocoa powder and xanthan gum (if using) and mix until a dough forms. Finally, add the choc chips and mix until evenly incorporated.
   Roll tablespoons of the dough into rounds and spread them out evenly on a baking tray lined with baking paper (see Tips). Press down on the balls to form discs and bake for 10–12 minutes, or until cracks have formed in the surface of the cookies.
   Cool on wire racks before eating – if you can wait that long! The cookies will keep in an airtight container at room temperature for up to 5 days.

Tip: If you have any loose choc chips after rolling the cookies, simply press them into the cookies before baking.

If you're looking for a slice to wow the masses, then look no further. This is simple to make and features homemade marshmallow. With just three ingredients – you read that right – you can make the most delicious, soft marshmallow that steals the show. The trick is to beat the ingredients for long enough, so set a timer and follow the directions closely.

Choc marshmallow slice

Prep time: 20 minutes
Cook time: 25 minutes
Serves: 8–10

Base
½ cup (125 g) butter, softened
¼ cup (55 g) caster (superfine) sugar
1¼ cups (185 g) gluten-free plain (all-purpose) flour
¼ teaspoon xanthan gum (omit if using regular flour)
½ cup (165 g) strawberry or raspberry jam

Marshmallow
2 tablespoons boiling water
½ tablespoon gelatin powder
½ cup (110 g) caster (superfine) sugar
2 tablespoons cold water

Topping
180 g (6½ oz) dark chocolate
3 teaspoons vegetable oil

Preheat the oven to 160°C (325°F). Grease and line a 23 × 23 cm (9 × 9 in) brownie tin with baking paper.

For the base, add the butter and sugar to a stand mixer fitted with the whisk attachment and beat until pale and fluffy, about 5 minutes. You can also do this by hand, just make sure your butter is nice and soft.

Add the flour and xanthan gum (if using) and mix to form a dough. Spread the dough evenly in the baking tray and bake for 25 minutes until lightly browned. The base will still be soft at this point, but it will harden as it cools. Once cooled, spread the jam over the base.

To make the marshmallow, combine the boiling water and gelatin in a bowl and mix to dissolve. Combine the sugar and cold water in the bowl of a stand mixer fitted with the whisk attachment and mix for 3 minutes on high speed. Add the gelatin mixture to the sugar mixture and beat for 8 minutes on high speed until it resembles a firm meringue. Spread the meringue evenly over the jam in the tin.

To make the topping, simply melt the chocolate and butter in the microwave in 30-second intervals, stirring after each interval, until melted. Spread the topping over the marshmallow (see Tip).

Refrigerate for 2 hours, or until the chocolate and marshmallow have set, then slice and enjoy. These will keep in an airtight container at room temperature for up to 1 week.

Tip: You can omit the chocolate topping layer and sprinkle with toasted shredded coconut for something a little different.

Melt in your mouth, buttery soft shortbread cookies – this recipe is so moreish, you will need all your willpower to not eat them all in one sitting (speaking from experience). The shortbread is very light, so handle the biscuits with care when sandwiching them together, as they can break easily – but these delicate treats are so worth the effort!

Melting moments with vanilla filling

Prep time: 15 minutes
Cook time: 12 minutes
Makes: 16

Shortbread

170 g (6 oz) butter, softened
30 g (1 oz) icing (confectioners')
 sugar, plus extra for dusting
1½ cups (220 g) gluten-free plain
 (all-purpose) flour, plus extra
 for dusting
30 g (1 oz) cornflour (cornstarch)
2 teaspoons xanthan gum (omit
 if using regular flour; see
 page 162)
1 teaspoon vanilla extract

Filling

1 cup (120 g) icing
 (confectioners') sugar
60 g (2 oz) butter, softened
2 teaspoons vanilla extract

Preheat the oven to 160°C (325°F).

For the shortbread, add the butter and sugar to a stand mixer fitted with the whisk attachment and cream together until thick and pale, about 5 minutes.

Sift in the flours and add the xanthan gum (if using) and vanilla extract. Gently mix until a soft dough forms. Take two teaspoons of the dough and roll into balls, then place on a lined baking tray. Once rolled, gently press with a fork to flatten. Bake for 10–12 minutes – they will look pale but they will be cooked. Allow to cool completely, as they are very crumbly when warm.

While the shortbread is cooling, cream all of the filling ingredients together in a stand mixer or by hand in a bowl until pale and the sugar has dissolved, about 5–8 minutes.

Sandwich the cookies together using about 1 teaspoon of the filling for each cookie. Be gentle when doing this, as the cookies are incredibly light and break easily.

Finally, dust with a little extra icing sugar to finish. Store in an airtight container at room temperature for up to 1 week. They will soften a little over time, but they'll still be delicious!

These are probably the easiest shortbread cookies you'll ever make, as they are simply mixed by hand in one bowl. Feel free to swap the chocolate chips for nuts or dried fruit, if you like. Get creative. Here, I've given you a couple of variations: one with choc chips and one with a strawberry glaze. I love these sorts of versatile recipes where you can vary the ingredients according to your taste.

Shortbread cookies two ways

Prep time: 30 minutes
Cook time: 20–30 minutes
Makes: 12

Shortbread cookies
125 g (4½ oz) gluten-free plain (all-purpose) flour
⅓ cup (40 g) cornflour (cornstarch)
1½ teaspoons xanthan gum (omit if using regular flour; see page 162)
60 g (2 oz) caster (superfine) sugar, plus extra for dusting (optional)
100 g (3½ oz) butter, cubed, at room temperature

Variation 1: choc chip
¼ cup (50 g) chocolate chips (milk, dark or white; see Tips)

Variation 2: strawberry glazed
⅓ cup (50 g) frozen strawberries (see Tips)
250 g (9 oz) icing (confectioners') sugar

For the shortbread cookies, add all the dry ingredients to a bowl. Add the butter and rub into the dry ingredients with your fingers until a dough forms.

If you're making choc chip cookies, mix in the choc chips now. I like to use my hands for this. If you're making strawberry glazed cookies, move on to the next step.

Place the dough on a large piece of baking paper and roll into a log, wrapping the dough in the paper and twisting both ends to tighten. Refrigerate for 15–30 minutes until cold.

Preheat the oven to 160°C (325°F).

Once the log is chilled, unwrap and slice into 2 cm (¾ in) thick cookies using a shape knife.

If you like, dip the rounds in some caster sugar as this will give them some extra crunch.

Bake for 20 minutes. The cookies will look pale and be soft, but they will harden as they cool. I find it best to leave them on the tray to cool, as they're more likely to break while warm.

If you're making the strawberry glaze (see Tips), place the frozen strawberries on a baking tray lined with baking paper and roast in the oven for 5–10 minutes, after you've baked the shortbread, until soft and juicy.

Add the strawberries and icing sugar to a stand mixer fitted with the whisk attachment and beat on high speed until smooth and the icing sugar has dissolved. Dip one half of the cooled cookies in the strawberry glaze, which will set will harden after a few minutes.

Store in an airtight container at room temperature for up to 1 week. They may soften a little over time but will still be delicious!

Tips: You can substitute nuts or dried fruit for the chocolate chips.

Use any frozen fruit you like to make the glaze. I have used raspberries and blueberries in the past, both of which work just as well. You can make this ahead of time and it will keep at room temperature for 2 days and in the fridge for 2 weeks. The colour will deepen and develop after a few hours, so if you want a stronger pink colour for your glaze, make this a few days ahead.

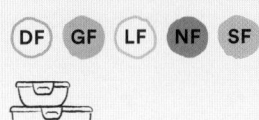

DF **GF** **LF** **NF** **SF**

This is the only brownie recipe you will ever need. You can add nuts, peanut butter, fruit, marshmallows – whatever you want – and consider this your new go-to base recipe that will work perfectly every time.

Chocolate brownies

Prep time: 5 minutes
Cook time: 40 minutes
Makes: 10–12

375 g (13 oz) butter, melted, plus extra for greasing (see Tip)
690 g (1 lb 9 oz) caster (superfine) sugar
6 eggs
½ tablespoon vanilla extract
330 g (11¾ oz) gluten-free plain (all-purpose) flour
113 g (4 oz) cocoa powder
1 teaspoon xanthan gum (omit if using regular flour; see page 162)

Preheat oven to 160°C (325°F). Grease and line a 33 × 23 cm (13 × 9 in) brownie tin with baking paper.

Add the butter and sugar to the bowl of a stand mixer fitted with the whisk attachment and beat on high speed for 3–4 minutes. Add the eggs, two at a time, mixing well after each addition.

Add the vanilla extract, flour, cocoa powder and xanthan gum (if using), and beat until mixed through.

Pour the mixture into the tin and bake for 40 minutes, or until the centre of the brownie is firm to the touch.

Allow to cool before slicing. These will keep at room temperature in an airtight container for up to 1 week, or they can be frozen in portions for up to 3 months. Simply allow to thaw at room temperature or reheat in the microwave for 1–2 minutes from frozen for a delicious gooey treat! Add some ice cream, too – trust me!

Tip: I have made these brownies with both dairy-free and regular butter, and they are both absolutely delicious!

This is an Aussie classic that has been a go-to slice of mine for years. You can find many variations of this slice, but this simple six-ingredient one is my favourite.

Passionfruit slice

Prep time: 10 minutes
Cook time: 25 minutes
Serves: 8–10

1 cup (220 g) caster (superfine) sugar
1 cup (90 g) desiccated coconut
1 cup (150 g) gluten-free self-raising flour
½ cup (125 g) butter, melted, plus extra for greasing
395 g (14 oz) tin sweetened condensed milk (see Tip)
170 g (6 oz) tin passionfruit pulp

Preheat the oven to 160°C (325°F). Grease and line a 23 × 23 cm (9 × 9 in) brownie tin with baking paper.

In a bowl, combine the sugar, coconut, flour and butter, and mix until a dough forms. Spread the dough in the bottom of the tin, pressing down firmly, then cook for 10–12 minutes, or until lightly golden. Allow the base to cool for 15–20 minutes.

Combine the condensed milk and passionfruit pulp in a bowl and pour on top of the base. Return to the oven and cook for another 10–12 minutes, or until the top is firm to touch.

Allow to cool, then refrigerate for 1–2 hours, or until set. Cut into bars or squares and store in an airtight container for up to 4 days at room temperature.

Tip: Substitute the sweetened condensed milk for sweetened condensed coconut milk to make it dairy free. You should be able to find this at your local supermarket.

Granola bars are so easy to make and are much healthier than store-bought versions. Use this as your base recipe and change the flavour by adding different nuts or seeds and even some dried fruit.

Healthy granola bars

Prep time: 15 minutes
Cook time: 30 minutes
Makes: 8–10

2 cups (195 g) quinoa flakes
1 cup (100 g) almond meal
½ cup (86 g) dark chocolate
   chips
½ cup (75 g) nuts or seeds
   of your choice (I like to use
   pepitas/pumpkin seeds)
½ cup (115 g) coconut oil, melted
½ cup (125 ml) pure maple syrup
½ teaspoon ground cinnamon
1 teaspoon vanilla extract

Preheat the oven to 180°C (350°F). Grease and line a 23 × 23 cm (9 × 9 in) brownie tin with baking paper.

Add all the ingredients to a bowl and mix until combined. Spread out in the tin and press down evenly. Bake for 25–30 minutes, or until golden brown.

Leave to cool, then cut into bars or squares. These will keep in an airtight container at room temperature for up to 5 days.

Perfect for any occasion, this slice is sure to impress! It has a rich, nutty flavour from the almond meal and a smooth, decadent filling that is contrasted by the crisp base and the sweetness of the jam.

Strawberry frangipane slice

Prep time: 15 minutes
Cook time: 1 hour 25 minutes
Serves: 10–12

Base
340 g (11¾ oz) gluten-free plain
   (all-purpose) flour
1 cup (125 g) icing
   (confectioners') sugar
220 g (7¾ oz) butter, softened

Filling
300 g (10½ oz) butter, softened
300 g (10½ oz) caster
   (superfine) sugar
2½ cups (250 g) almond meal
1 egg
pinch of salt
1 tablespoon milk of your choice
½ cup (165 g) strawberry jam
¼ cup (25 g) flaked almonds,
   for topping

Preheat the oven to 170°C (350°F) and line a 23 × 33 cm (9 × 13 in) baking tray with baking paper.

Mix all the ingredients for the base together and press firmly into the base of the tin. Bake for 15 minutes, then remove and allow to cool.

For the filling, put the butter and sugar in a stand mixer fitted with the whisk attachment and beat together until light and fluffy, about 5 minutes. Add the almond meal, egg and salt, and mix until incorporated. Add the milk and beat for another 1–2 minutes.

Once the base has cooled, spread the jam on top, then spread over the filling mixture. Bake for 1 hour to 1 hour 10 minutes, or until golden brown. Halfway through cooking, sprinkle the flaked almonds on the top of the slice. These need to be added at the halfway point otherwise they will burn.

Allow to cool completely before cutting into bars or squares. Store in an airtight container at room temperature or in the fridge for up to 4 days.

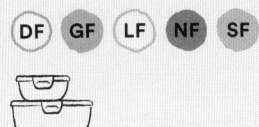

DF GF LF NF SF

A blondie is the sister of a brownie. While both are made with butter, sugar, flour and eggs, blondies use brown sugar and don't have cocoa powder, which results in a delicious vanilla batter with caramel undertones. They are dense, chewy and strike the perfect balance of sweet and salty with the use of salted butter. Add some ice cream for extra indulgence!

Raspberry white choc blondies

Prep time: 10 minutes
Cook time: 35 minutes
Makes: 10–12

170 g (6 oz) salted butter, melted
225 g (8 oz) soft brown sugar
1 egg
2 teaspoons vanilla extract
210 g (7½ oz) gluten-free plain (all-purpose) flour
⅔ cup (100 g) white chocolate chips
50 g (1¾ oz) frozen or fresh raspberries

Preheat the oven to 160°C (325°F) and line a 20 × 20 cm (8 × 8 in) baking tray with baking paper.

Mix the melted butter and brown sugar in a bowl for 1–2 minutes, then add the egg and combine. Add the vanilla and flour, and mix to make a batter. Add the white chocolate chips and raspberries and fold through until combined. Bake for 30–35 minutes.

Leave to cool before cutting into squares. These will keep at room temperature in an airtight container for up to 1 week, or they can be frozen in portions for up to 3 months. Simply allow to thaw at room temperature or reheat in the microwave for 1–2 minutes from frozen for a delicious gooey treat.

If you're like me, dessert time is your favourite time, but nothing ruins a sweet treat like feeling ill afterwards. When I was first on the low-FODMAP diet, I used to either sneak in a piece of cake and suffer afterwards or just skip dessert altogether. Well, these are no longer your only options! With the recipes in this section, you can not only eat dessert but enjoy it worry free and, best of all, symptom free! From comforting rice pudding to show-stopping red velvet cake, there is something here for every occasion. Now you can bring back cake time with confidence and a happy tummy!

Have Your Cake and Eat It Too

(Minus the Bloat!)

These fluffy, golden scrolls are generously swirled with a sweet cinnamon-sugar filling and topped with a luscious glaze, making them the perfect indulgence for breakfast, brunch or any time you crave a comforting snack.

Cinnamon scrolls

Prep time: 30 minutes
Cook time: 12 minutes
Makes: 6

½ cup (125 ml) warm water
1 × 7 g (¼ oz) packet instant
   dried yeast
340 g (11¾ oz) gluten-free plain
   (all-purpose) flour, plus extra
   for dusting
1 teaspoon xanthan gum
   (omit if using regular flour;
   see page 162)
35 g (1¼ oz) caster (superfine)
   sugar, plus 1 teaspoon extra
1 teaspoon ground cinnamon
½ teaspoon salt
1 teaspoon vanilla extract
100 ml (3½ fl oz) milk of your
   choice
1 egg

Filling
2 tablespoons butter, softened
½ cup (110 g) soft brown sugar
1 tablespoon ground cinnamon

Glaze
1½ cups (185 g) icing
   (confectioners') sugar
2 tablespoons milk of your choice
¼ teaspoon vanilla extract
1 tablespoon butter

To make the dough, add the warm water, yeast and the extra teaspoon of sugar to a large bowl and allow to sit for 10–15 minutes for the yeast to activate. It should get frothy.

Once the mixture is frothy, sift in the flour, xanthan gum (if using), sugar, cinnamon and salt and add the vanilla extract, milk and egg. Mix until a dough is formed. You can also do this in a stand mixer fitted with the paddle attachment (although be aware that the dough hook doesn't work as well with gluten-free flour). If you're using regular wheat flour, allow the dough to rest for 30 minutes.

Dust your benchtop with flour and turn out the dough. Knead until smooth, about 2–3 minutes. Dust the bench with more flour and roll out the dough into a 30 × 23 cm (12 × 9 in) rectangle.

For the filling, spread the softened butter over the surface of the dough. Combine the brown sugar and cinnamon in a small bowl and mix thoroughly, then sprinkle evenly over the butter.

Gently roll the dough up from the longer side into a log, then cut into 5 cm (2 in) pieces.

Place the scrolls on a baking tray lined with baking paper. If using gluten-free flour, it's best to pack them tightly, so a smaller tray works best. Otherwise, if you're using regular wheat flour, place the scrolls about 2 cm (¾ in) apart on a larger tray to allow them to rise in the oven.

Preheat the oven to 180°C (350°F).

Allow the scrolls to rest in a warm, dark place for 20–30 minutes. They should rise and be touching each other.

Bake for 10–12 minutes, or until slightly browned.

While the scrolls are baking, make the glaze by mixing all the ingredients together, either in a stand mixer fitted with the whisk attachment, or in a bowl with a hand beater, until the sugar has dissolved and the glaze has lightened in colour, about 3–4 minutes.

Once the scrolls are cooked, allow to cool for 5–10 minutes before spreading the glaze generously over the top. Serve warm.

Tip: These are best consumed the day they are made, but if you do have leftovers, store them in an airtight container at room temperature for up to 2 days and reheat in the microwave for 15 seconds to warm through and soften before eating.

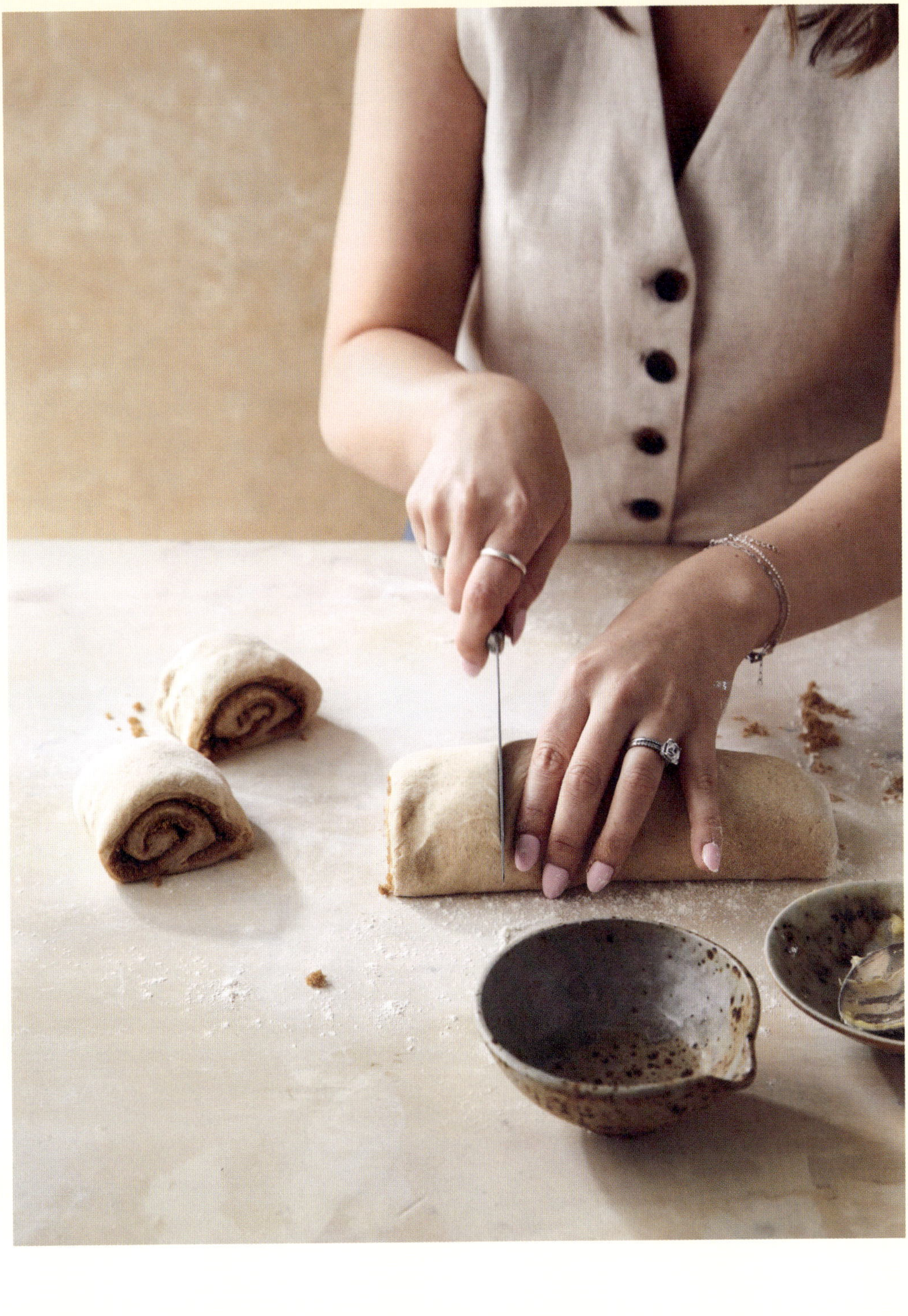

Honestly, these are the lightest and fluffiest cupcakes you will ever make. They are truly delightful! The trick is all in the extra baking powder, which gives them extra rise and an airy texture. I have made these countless times and they are almost too moreish. It's difficult to stop at just one.

The best vanilla cupcakes with vanilla buttercream

Prep time: 15 minutes
Cook time: 15 minutes
Makes: 20

Cupcakes
1 cup (250 g) butter, softened
290 g (10¼ oz) caster
   (superfine) sugar
230 g (8 oz) gluten-free
   self-raising flour
30 g (1 oz) baking powder
2 teaspoons xanthan gum
   (omit if using regular flour;
   see page 162)
½ cup (125 ml) milk of your
   choice
30 ml (1 fl oz) vanilla extract
4 eggs

Buttercream
500 g (1 lb 2 oz) icing
   (confectioners') sugar
240 g (8½ oz) salted butter,
   softened (see Tips)
2 tablespoons vanilla extract

Preheat the oven to 180°C (350°F) or 160°C (315°F) fan forced. Line two 12-hole muffin tins with cupcake cases.

For the cupcakes, add the butter and sugar to a stand mixer fitted with the paddle attachment and beat for 4–5 minutes until light and fluffy. You can also do this by hand.

Sift in the flour, baking powder and xanthan gum (if using), then add the milk, vanilla extract and eggs. Gently fold through until everything is well combined and a batter has formed.

Fill the cupcake cases halfway with the batter (if you fill them more than halfway, they will overflow as they cook). Bake for 10–15 minutes, or until golden brown and a skewer in the middle of one cupcake comes out clean. Transfer to a wire rack to cool.

While the cupcakes are cooling, make the buttercream. Simply beat all the ingredients in a stand mixer fitted with the paddle attachment, or in a mixing bowl with an electric mixer, until the sugar has dissolved and the buttercream is white and fluffy, 5–10 minutes.

Allow the cupcakes to cool completely before icing with the buttercream. Store in an airtight container for 3–4 days.

Tips: I like to use salted butter for the buttercream, as it cuts through the sweetness a little. If you don't have it, then add a pinch of salt. It does make it more balanced.

To make these into chocolate cupcakes, simply add 50 g (1¾ oz) cocoa powder with the flour. You can also make a chocolate buttercream by adding 80 g (2¾ oz) cocoa powder to the icing. Just be sure to sift the cocoa powder, as it's notoriously lumpy!

These mug cakes can be made in the oven or the microwave and are a healthier take on traditional mug cakes, as they don't contain any oil or butter. I love to make them when I am craving something sweet. They're perfect served with ice cream.

Quick gooey mug cakes

Prep time: 10 minutes
Cook time: 3–15 minutes
Serves: 2

extra-virgin olive oil or butter,
    for greasing
1 banana, mashed
⅓ cup (50 g) gluten-free
    self-raising flour
40 g (1½ oz) almond meal
1½ tablespoons pure maple
    syrup
1½ tablespoons cocoa powder
1 teaspoon baking powder
⅓ cup (80 ml) milk of your
    choice
20 g (¾ oz) dark chocolate
    squares or buttons

If using the oven, preheat to 180°C (350°F) and grease two ovenproof ramekins with oil or butter.

Combine all the ingredients, except the chocolate, in a bowl and mix until a batter has formed, then divide between the two ramekins.

Press half the chocolate into the centre of each cake, making sure they are well covered with batter. This will make a gooey centre once cooked. Bake for 12–15 minutes, or you can microwave them for 2–3 minutes (see Tip). Eat straight away.

Tip: If you're using a microwave, make sure to use a tall mug to avoid the cake spilling over, as it will rise during the cooking process.

Indulge in the exquisite blend of tangy and sweet with this lemon meringue cheesecake, featuring a luscious lemon curd. This delightful dessert marries the creamy richness of a classic cheesecake with the vibrant zing of fresh lemon. It's topped with a light, fluffy meringue that's gently toasted to perfection. It has become one of my most requested desserts to bring to family gatherings, and I have no doubt the same will happen with your families.

The recipe does have a few steps to it, but it is 100 per cent worth the bit of extra work. You will also need a blowtorch for the meringue – unfortunately, as this is a no-bake cheesecake, it cannot go in the oven to cook the meringue, as it will melt the cheesecake filling.

No-bake lemon curd and lemon meringue cheesecake

Prep time: 30 minutes
Cook time: 10 minutes
Serves: 12

extra-virgin olive oil or butter,
	for greasing

Lemon curd
1½ tablespoons cornflour
	(cornstarch)
zest of 1 lemon
juice of 3 lemons (approx.
	200 ml/7 fl oz)
3 egg yolks (save the whites for
	the meringue)
125 g (4½ oz) caster (superfine)
	sugar

Base
400 g (14 oz) packet gluten-free
	plain sweet meal biscuits
100 g (3½ oz) butter, melted,
	plus extra if needed

Grease a 24 cm (9½ in) springform cake tin with oil or butter.

To make the curd, mix the cornflour with the lemon juice and zest in a bowl. In another bowl, whisk the egg yolks and sugar until well combined.

Heat 225 ml (7¾ fl oz) water over high heat until just starting to boil. The cornflour will settle at the bottom of the bowl, so give the mixture a quick stir before adding it to the boiling water with the lemon. Whisk continuously until thick, about 2–3 minutes. Once the mixture has thickened, remove it from the heat and leave to cool for 1 minute.

Add some of the egg yolk and sugar mixture to the lemon mixture and stir quickly to combine, then add the remaining egg yolk and sugar mixture.

Once everything is combined, place the pan back over medium–high heat and stir until thickened, about another 2–3 minutes. Remove from the heat and leave to cool completely. The curd will keep in an airtight container for 1–2 weeks in the fridge, so you can make this ahead of time.

For the cheesecake base, blitz the biscuits and melted butter together in a food processor until a crumb forms (add a little more melted butter if needed). Press the crumb mixture into the base of the tin. Use a glass to press and compact the crumb firmly, making sure to even out the edges where the base and side meets, as it can get quite thick. Refrigerate until set.

→

Filling

2 teaspoons gelatin powder

¼ cup (60 ml) lemon juice

500 g (1 lb 2 oz) cream cheese, softened

¾ cup (165 g) caster (superfine) sugar

zest of 1 lemon

½ cup (125 g) sour cream

1 cup (250 ml) thick (double/heavy) cream

Meringue

3 egg whites (reserved from the curd)

¾ cup (165 g) caster (superfine) sugar

For the filling, in a small saucepan, sprinkle the gelatin over the lemon juice and let it sit for a couple of minutes. Turn the heat to low and warm, stirring constantly until the gelatin has dissolved. Allow to cool slightly.

Add the cream cheese and sugar to a stand mixer fitted with the whisk attachment and beat until smooth and creamy. You can also do this in a large mixing bowl with an electric mixer. Add the lemon zest, lemon juice mixture and sour cream and beat until combined. Pour in the cream and beat for 2–3 minutes, or until fluffy.

Pour the filling on top of the base and refrigerate for at least 2 hours, or overnight, to set.

Once set, spread the lemon curd on top about 1–2 cm (½–¾ in) thick. The thicker the layer, the tangier your cheesecake will be.

Make the meringue on the day you wish to serve. Place the egg whites and sugar in a small saucepan set over low heat. Stir continuously until the sugar has dissolved and the whites look a little frothy. Remove from the heat and allow to cool slightly before whipping to stiff peaks in a stand mixer fitted with the whisk attachment, or by hand with an electric mixer.

Spoon on top of the cheesecake and toast the meringue with a blowtorch until it is nice and golden all over.

Rizogalo means 'rice milk' in Greek, and it's a creamy, dreamy dessert made with tender rice gently simmered in milk and sweetened to perfection. Infused with a hint of vanilla and dusted with cinnamon, this classic treat offers a delicate balance of flavours and a luscious, velvety texture. Eat warm or cold.

Rizogalo
Rice pudding

Prep time: 5 minutes
Cook time: 30 minutes
Serves: 4

½ cup (100 g) medium-grain white rice
4 cups (1 litre) milk of your choice (see Tip)
40 g (1½ oz) caster (superfine) sugar
1 teaspoon vanilla extract
½ teaspoon ground cinnamon or 1 cinnamon stick, plus extra ground cinnamon, for dusting

Add all the ingredients to a saucepan and bring to the boil over medium heat, stirring continuously. Be careful not to allow the mixture to boil rapidly, otherwise it will spill over the edge of the pan. Once it starts bubbling, reduce the heat to low, cover and simmer for 20–30 minutes, or until the rice is cooked. The mixture should still be a little runny, as it will thicken as it cools.

Pour into four individual ceramic ramekins, bowls or cups, and sprinkle some extra ground cinnamon on top.

You can eat this warm or cold. If eating warm, allow to cool for 15 minutes before consuming as it will be too hot. Store in an airtight container in the fridge for up to 4 days.

Tip: If using plant-based milk, I recommend a soy or macadamia milk for this recipe as these have a creamier, thicker texture than almond or rice milk, which tend to be more watery in consistency.

The perfect blend of tart and sweet with a slightly nutty crust, this tart is a winner on all fronts. Make this and everyone will not only be impressed but lining up for more!

Simple rhubarb tart

Prep time: 10 minutes
Cook time: 35 minutes
Serves: 12

yoghurt of choice, to serve
  (optional)

Crust
100 g (3½ oz) butter, softened,
  plus extra for greasing
1 egg
50 g (1¾ oz) caster (superfine)
  sugar
1 teaspoon vanilla extract
1 cup (150 g) gluten-free plain
  (all-purpose) flour
125 g (4½ oz) almond meal

Filling
600 g (1 lb 5 oz) fresh or frozen
  rhubarb, chopped (see Tip)
200 g (7 oz) caster (superfine)
  sugar
3 teaspoons lemon juice
1 tablespoon gelatin powder

Preheat the oven to 180°C (350°F) and grease a 22 cm (8½ in) pie tin or dish with butter.

Add all the crust ingredients to a bowl and mix until a dough forms. You can use your hands if easier.

Press the dough into the pie tin using your hands, spreading it evenly on the bottom and up the sides. Then, with a measuring cup or glass, press down firmly to smooth out the dough. Prick the base of the dough with a fork a few times, then bake for 20 minutes, or until golden brown. Remove and leave to cool.

To make the filling, add all the ingredients to a saucepan with ¾ cup (185 ml) water and cook over medium–high heat until the rhubarb is soft, 10–15 minutes. Purée with a hand-held blender and pour into the cooled pie crust.

Allow to cool before refrigerating for 2 hours, or overnight, to let the filling set.

Serve dolloped with yoghurt, if desired.

Tip: You can use a muffin tin to make mini tarts if you don't have a larger pie tin or want individual serves. Line the muffin tins with rounds of pastry, pour in the rhubarb purée and bake for 5–10 minutes.

Your tart may vary in colour depending on the rhubarb's ripeness.

There's no better show-stopping cake than red velvet. Rich and decadent, this cake has an undeniable allure, but the real star of this recipe is the traditional cooked frosting. Creamy, silky and fluffy, this frosting is lighter than regular buttercream and not as sweet, bringing the perfect balance to the cake's rich flavours. Don't just take my word for it – try it for yourself and taste the difference!

Red velvet cake with creamy frosting

Prep time: 15 minutes
Cook time: 55 minutes
Serves: 12

Cake

2½ cups (375 g) gluten-free
plain (all-purpose) flour
1½ cups (330 g) caster
(superfine) sugar
1 teaspoon xanthan gum
(omit if using regular flour;
see page 162)
2 tablespoons cocoa powder
1 tablespoon baking powder
1 teaspoon salt
1½ cups (375 ml) vegetable oil
1 cup (250 ml) buttermilk
(see Tip)
1 × 50 ml (1¾ fl oz) bottle red
food colouring
2 eggs

Creamy frosting

1½ cups (330 g) caster
(superfine) sugar
1½ cups (375 ml) milk of your
choice
½ cup (70 g) gluten-free plain
(all-purpose) flour
300 g (10½ oz) butter, softened
2 teaspoons vanilla extract

Preheat the oven to 180°C (350°F) and grease and line a 24 cm (9½ in) round springform cake tin with baking paper.

In a bowl, beat all the cake ingredients together until a smooth batter has formed. Pour into the cake tin and bake for 45–55 minutes, or until a skewer inserted in the middle of the cake comes out clean. Leave to cool in the tin for a few minutes, then turn out onto a wire rack and leave to cool completely.

Meanwhile, add the sugar, milk and flour to a saucepan and heat over medium heat, whisking continuously until the mixture has thickened to a pudding-like consistency. Remove from the heat and allow to cool completely.

Put the butter in a stand mixer fitted with the whisk attachment and beat on high speed until light and fluffy, about 5 minutes. You can also do this by hand. Add the sugar mixture, 1 tablespoon at a time, beating well after each addition, then add the vanilla extract. Continue to beat on high speed until the frosting is smooth and fluffy.

To decorate, cut the cake in half horizontally and spread half the frosting over the middle of the cake and the remaining half on top of the cake.

Tip: You can make your own buttermilk by adding 1 tablespoon lemon juice or white vinegar to milk of your choice and leaving it to stand for 10 minutes. This will work for any milk.

A mud cake is an Australian classic: dense, rich and oh so chocolatey! I like to use milk and butter in the ganache instead of cream so it can be more easily substituted for dairy-free alternatives, but this does make it a little softer, so remember to refrigerate the cake before serving to set the icing.

Chocolate mud cake

Prep time: 10 minutes
Cook time: 40 minutes
Serves: 12

240 g (8½ oz) caster (superfine)
  sugar
100 g (3½ oz) butter softened,
  plus extra for greasing
200 g (7 oz) dark chocolate chips
240 g (8½ oz) gluten-free
  self-raising flour
1 teaspoon xanthan gum
  (omit if using regular flour;
  see page 162)
20 g (¾ oz) cocoa powder
1 teaspoon baking powder
3 g (⅛ oz/½ teaspoon) salt
2 eggs
2 teaspoons vanilla extract
1 cup (250 g) yoghurt of your
  choice

Ganache
⅔ cup (100 g) dark chocolate
  chips
50 g (1¾ oz) butter
30–60 ml (1–2 fl oz) milk of
  your choice

Preheat the oven to 180°C (350°F). Grease a 30 cm (12 in) round springform cake tin with baking paper.

Add the sugar and butter to a stand mixer fitted with the whisk attachment and beat until pale and fluffy, about 3–4 minutes. You can also do this in a large mixing bowl with an electric mixer.

Melt the chocolate chips in the microwave in 30-second intervals, then allow to cool slightly.

Sift the flour, xanthan gum (if using), cocoa powder, baking powder and salt into the butter and sugar mixture. Add the melted chocolate, eggs, vanilla extract and yoghurt and mix until a batter has formed. Pour into the tin and bake for 30–40 minutes, or until a skewer inserted in the middle of the cake comes out clean. Allow the cake to cool completely.

To make the ganache, add the chocolate and butter to a heatproof bowl. Heat the milk in a saucepan or in the microwave until hot. Pour the hot milk over the chocolate and butter and allow to sit for 30 seconds, then mix until the chocolate has melted.

Allow the ganache to cool before pouring on top of the cake. This ganache is softer than those made with cream, so refrigerate the cake for 20 minutes before serving to let the ganache set.

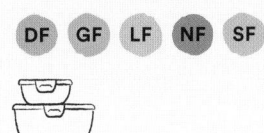

DF GF LF NF SF

This delightful recipe combines the natural sweetness of ripe bananas with a moist, tender crumb that makes a loaf perfect for any time of day. Whether you're enjoying a slice for breakfast, an afternoon snack or a simple dessert, this banana bread delivers rich flavour and warm, cosy vibes in every bite. Best of all, it comes together in a snap, making it an ideal treat for busy days when you're craving something freshly baked.

Simple banana bread

Prep time: 5 minutes
Cook time: 45 minutes
Serves: 12

285 g (10¼ oz) gluten-free
  self-raising flour
200 g (7 oz) caster (superfine)
  sugar
1¼ teaspoons baking powder
2 g (⅙ oz) salt
1 teaspoon xanthan gum
  (omit if using regular flour;
  see page 162)
½ cup (125 ml) vegetable oil,
  plus extra for greasing
3 eggs
1 teaspoon vanilla extract
235 g (8½ oz/approx. 2)
  bananas, peeled and mashed

Preheat the oven to 180°C (350°F). Grease and line a standard loaf (bar) tin with baking paper.

Combine all the ingredients in a bowl and mix well to form a batter. Pour into the tin and bake for 45 minutes, or until a skewer inserted in the middle of the loaf comes out clean.

Allow to cool before slicing. This can be stored in an airtight container at room temperature for up to 5 days or can frozen in slices for up to 3 months. I like wrap each slice in some plastic wrap before freezing, which helps to keep the slices from sticking together. To thaw, simply leave out at room temperature or heat in the microwave for 1–2 minutes from frozen.

Tip: I like to pop a slice in the toaster to get a little crunchy, then top with some salted butter or chocolate hazelnut spread – or both!

The secret to tasty low-FODMAP food is to add extra flavour where you can, either with a dipping sauce or an extra-tasty dressing. These recipes are simple staples that will elevate any standard meal to new heights. For example, by learning how to make a classic mayonnaise, you can create all kinds of sauces and spreads that will enhance any dish. So, sauce it up with these foundational recipes and be kind to your stomach at the same time.

Don't Miss Out On Flavour:

Basics You Can Trust

Whole-egg mayonnaise

One recipe to rule them all! Making whole-egg mayonnaise is so quick and easy, you'll be wondering why you ever bought it from a supermarket. This can be made in a stand mixer with the whisk attachment, in a hand-held blender or even by hand if you feel so inclined (although you may need to enlist some assistance to give your arm a rest!). Using this recipe as a base, you can make endless flavour combinations, such as garlic (see opposite), chilli and lime (see opposite) and maple dijon (see right).

Prep time: 5 minutes
Cook time: Nil
Makes: 2 cups (600 g)

2 eggs
2 teaspoons dijon mustard
1 tablespoon white vinegar
2 cups (500 ml) vegetable oil
salt and black pepper, to taste

Add all the ingredients, except the oil, to a blender or mixer. Blend until well combined, then add the oil in a very steady stream, mixing continuously until thick and creamy.

Store in an airtight container or bottle in the fridge for up to 2 weeks.

Maple dijon mayonnaise

Not to sound like a broken record, but the basic Whole-egg mayonnaise (see left) really is the master of all! For a delicious sweet and tangy mayo that is amazing on burgers, get a bottle of this variation in your fridge.

Prep time: 5 minutes
Cook time: Nil
Makes: approx. 2 cups (600 g)

1 tablespoon dijon mustard
1½ tablespoons pure maple syrup
1 quantity Whole-egg mayonnaise (see left)

Add the mustard and maple syrup to the mayonnaise and mix well.

Store in an airtight container or bottle in the fridge for up to 2 weeks.

Cheat's aioli

Aioli is simply garlic and oil and, depending on who you ask, is either garlicky mayo or mashed garlic emulsified with oil. Personally, I've always considered it garlicky mayo, so here is my cheat's version. I call it cheat's as we won't be using actual garlic for obvious reasons (it's not LoFo, duh!) but garlic-infused olive oil instead. It's simply the same as my Whole-egg mayonnaise (see opposite) with a splash of garlic oil and lemon juice added.

Prep time: 5 minutes
Cook time: Nil
Makes: approx. 2 cups (600 g)

2 tablespoons garlic-infused olive oil
2 teaspoons lemon juice
1 quantity Whole-egg mayonnaise (see opposite)

Add the garlic oil and lemon juice to the mayonnaise and mix well. Store in an airtight container or bottle in the fridge for up to 2 weeks.

Chilli lime aioli

There's something about the bright zing of lime paired with the subtle heat of chilli that transforms a simple aioli into a stand-out condiment. This chilli lime aioli is the perfect companion to everything from crispy fries to grilled seafood, bringing a burst of flavour to every bite. It's creamy and tangy, with just the right amount of spice to keep your tastebuds intrigued. Whether you're looking to elevate your tacos, spice up a burger or simply dip your veggies into something delicious, this versatile aioli is sure to become a staple in your kitchen.

Prep time: 5 minutes
Cook time: Nil
Makes: approx. 2 cups (600 g)

zest of ½ lime
juice of 1 lime, or to taste
2 teaspoons chilli flakes, or to taste
1 quantity Whole-egg mayonnaise (see opposite)

Add the lime zest and juice, and the chilli flakes, to the mayonnaise and mix well. Store in an airtight container or bottle in the fridge for up to 2 weeks.

Clockwise from left: Whole-egg mayonnaise; Miso dressing; mustard; Chilli lime aioli; Maple dijon mayonnaise

Basil pesto

It really is so simple to make your own pesto, and I guarantee this version will soon become your favourite way to bring an extra layer of flavour to any dish. I like to use baby spinach and rocket (arugula) in my pesto to bulk it out so that you get a higher yield per bunch of basil.

Prep time: 5 minutes
Cook time: Nil
Makes: 1 cup (250 g)

25–30 g (1 oz) fresh basil leaves
40 g (1½ oz) baby spinach
⅓ cup (15 g) rocket (arugula)
1 tablespoon garlic-infused olive oil
2–3 tablespoons extra-virgin olive oil
1 tablespoon lemon juice
½ teaspoon salt
25 g (1 oz) toasted pine nuts
10 g (¼ oz) grated parmesan cheese
   (omit if making this dairy free)

Simply add all the ingredients to a blender and blitz until smooth.

This recipe makes about 1 cup (250 g), but feel free to double it and make more, as it freezes well in ice-cube trays for up to 3 months, ready to add to things like pastas, soups and dressings. To thaw, leave in the fridge overnight or microwave in 30-second intervals.

Kale pesto

This is a great alternative to Basil pesto (see left) and is perfect for anyone who is dairy or nut free. Basil pesto can be a little overpowering; this recipe is great if you're looking for something with a subtler flavour but still want to add colour and zing to a dish. It's great as a salad dressing and as a dip.

Prep time: 5 minutes
Cook time: Nil
Makes: ½ cup (125 g)

40 g (1½ oz) kale leaves (see Tip)
⅓ cup (15 g) rocket (arugula)
15 g (½ oz) toasted pepitas (pumpkin seeds)
⅓ cup (80 ml) extra-virgin olive oil
3 teaspoons lemon juice
2 teaspoons garlic-infused olive oil
½ teaspoon salt

Add all the ingredients to a food processor and blend until smooth.

Freeze the pesto in ice-cube trays for up to 3 months. The small quantities make it easy to add to soups, dressings or pasta sauces. To thaw, leave in the fridge overnight or microwave in 30-second intervals.

Tip: Massage the kale leaves for 1–2 minutes to make them more tender. You can do this any time you're using kale to make it less chewy and bitter.

L–R: Basil pesto; Kale pesto

A tangy yet sweet dressing that works beautifully with salads. This dressing also keeps well in the fridge for a couple of weeks, so feel free to make extra. It's great drizzled on top of the rainbow salad (page 108). Unlike other dressings, this one is cooked on the stove, but it's well worth this extra step.

Miso dressing

Prep time: 5 minutes
Cook time: 5 minutes
Makes: ½ cup (125 ml)

1 tablespoon white miso paste
¼ cup (60 ml) pure maple syrup
¼ cup (60 ml) lemon juice
2 teaspoons garlic-infused
   olive oil
1 teaspoon soy sauce
1 teaspoon sesame oil
1 teaspoon rice-wine vinegar

Place all the ingredients in a saucepan with ¼ cup (60 ml) water and bring to the boil over medium–high heat, then reduce the heat to low and simmer for 3–5 minutes. Allow to cool, then store in an airtight container or bottle in the fridge for up to 3 weeks.

Every time I make this dressing, people ask me for the recipe. Even on a simple garden salad, it's a winner. It's got the perfect amount of tang without overpowering other flavours, and turns any salad into a show stopper.

The best balsamic dressing

Prep time: 5 minutes
Cook time: Nil
Makes: 150 ml (5 fl oz)

½ cup (125 ml) extra-virgin
   olive oil
1½ tablespoons balsamic vinegar
2 teaspoons dijon mustard
½ teaspoon salt
¼ teaspoon black pepper

Add all the ingredients to a bowl and mix or whisk until combined. You can also add everything to a jar, put the lid on and shake. Alternatively, you can use a hand-held blender, which will nicely emulsify the dressing.

Store in an airtight container or bottle in the fridge for 2–3 weeks. Just be sure to give it a good whisk or shake before using as the oil and vinegar can separate.

If you want to take your basic dressing to a new level, then this is the perfect recipe. It's great for use in 'fancier' salads, such as those with grains, nuts or seeds and roasted vegetables, as it works perfectly with more robust flavours, but it's also amazing with simple greens.

Sweet and tangy maple dijon dressing

Prep time: 5 minutes
Cook time: Nil
Makes: 150 ml (5 fl oz)

½ cup (125 ml) extra-virgin
  olive oil
1½ tablespoons balsamic vinegar
1 tablespoon dijon mustard
3 teaspoons pure maple syrup
½ teaspoon salt
¼ teaspoon black pepper

Add all the ingredients to a bowl and mix or whisk until combined. You can also add everything to a jar, put the lid on and shake. Alternatively, you can use a hand-held blender, which will nicely emulsify the dressing.

Store in an airtight container or bottle in the fridge for 2–3 weeks. Just be sure to give it a good whisk or shake before using, as the oil and vinegar can separate.

Olive tapenade is a great addition to any mezze platter, as it works so well as a dip with toasted bread or pita bread. I also like to add it to salads, wraps and pasta – pretty much anything that needs a salty hit.

Simple olive tapenade

Prep time: 5 minutes
Cook time: Nil
Makes: ½ cup (125 g)

100 g (3½ oz) pitted kalamata (black) olives
10 g (¼ oz) capers
1 tablespoon flat-leaf (Italian) parsley
2 teaspoons lemon juice
1 teaspoon garlic-infused olive oil
½ teaspoon black pepper
2 tablespoons extra-virgin olive oil

Add all the ingredients to a blender or food processor and pulse until coarsely chopped.

Store in an airtight container in the fridge for 2–3 weeks.

You will be pleased to know that tinned chickpeas are low FODMAP at ¼ cup (40 g) per serve. You can enjoy this recipe bloat free, but don't be tempted to eat the whole batch – no matter how delicious it is! This recipe is also a great way to incorporate some more fibre into your diet. I love this as a dip as well as a spread on toast or added to salads.

Roasted carrot hummus

Prep time: 10 minutes
Cook time: 40 minutes
Makes: 2 cups (440 g)

500 g (1 lb 5 oz) carrot,
    peeled and cut into 2–3 cm
    (¾–1¼ in) thick rounds
1 teaspoon salt
½ teaspoon black pepper
3 teaspoons garlic-infused
    olive oil
160 g (5¾ oz) tinned chickpeas,
    drained and rinsed well
3 teaspoons tahini
1 tablespoon extra-virgin olive oil
3 teaspoons lemon juice

Preheat the oven to 180°C (350°F).

Put the carrot on a baking tray and season with the salt, pepper and garlic oil. Roast for 30–40 minutes until soft, then allow to cool.

Once cooled, add the carrot to a blender or food processor with all the other ingredients and blitz until smooth.

Store in an airtight container in the fridge for up to 4 days.

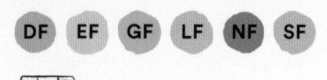

This is my staple tomato sauce. You will see this recipe featured in a few recipes in this book, as it's so versatile and an easy substitute for ready-made pasta sauce (since they are generally not low FODMAP).

Napoli sauce

Prep time: 5 minutes
Cook time: 20 minutes
Makes: about 3 cups (750 g)

2 × 400 g (14 oz) tins tomatoes
2 tablespoons garlic-infused
  olive oil
1 tablespoon dried basil
1 tablespoon dried oregano
1 teaspoon salt
½ teaspoon black pepper
1 teaspoon dried chives
1 teaspoon caster sugar
  (optional)

Put the tinned tomatoes in a blender and blitz until smooth, or you can use a hand-held blender.

Add to a saucepan with all the other ingredients and bring to the boil, then reduce the heat to low and simmer for 20 minutes.

Store in an airtight container in the fridge up to a week or in portions in the freezer for up to 3 months. Thaw in the microwave for 2–3 minutes or defrost in a saucepan pan over low heat.

Beef stock is a little more involved than chicken stock (page 217), but it's well worth the extra effort to have homemade stock stashed away in the fridge or freezer. The bones are roasted before simmering in water, which adds lots of deep umami flavour to the final stock. Just like the chicken stock, you can add whatever left-over vegetables you have on hand and some aromatics, such as bay leaves, peppercorns and thyme. Apple-cider vinegar helps to break down the cartilage and marrow so you get even more nutrients into your stock, and it doesn't affect the flavour at all.

Low-FODMAP beef stock

Prep time: 1 hour
Cook time: 6–9 hours
Makes: 4 cups (1 litre)

1.5–2 kg (3 lb 5 oz–4 lb 8 oz)
   beef bones
1 carrot, quartered
60 g (2 oz) fennel
40 g (1½ oz) spring onion
   (scallion) tops
3 bay leaves
30 g (1 oz) flat-leaf (Italian)
   parsley sprigs
½ tablespoon black peppercorns
½ tablespoon dried or fresh
   thyme
2 teaspoons salt
1 tablespoon apple-cider vinegar
½ tablespoon garlic-infused
   olive oil (optional)
8 cups (2 litres) cold water

Preheat the oven to 220°C (425°F).

Lay the beef bones in a roasting tin and roast for 1 hour, turning halfway through.

Once the bones are browned, add to a large stockpot with all the other ingredients.

Discard the fat left over in the roasting tin, but deglaze the tin by adding some hot water and placing the tin over low heat or back in the oven for a few minutes to melt those caramelised juices. Scrape them with a spatula and add to the stockpot. This will add lots of extra flavour.

Place the pot over medium–high heat and bring to the boil. As soon as it starts bubbling, reduce the heat to low and simmer uncovered for 5–8 hours, topping up the water as needed to keep the bones submerged.

Remove the large bones and drain the stock through a colander set over a bowl. Discard the solids.

Allow the stock to cool before refrigerating. After a couple hours in the fridge, a hardened layer of fat will have formed on the surface of the stock. Remove and discard it, or reserve it for cooking with, as it contains quite a lot of flavour. Underneath you should have a beautiful, gelatinous stock.

Store in the fridge for up to 5 days, or in portions in the freezer for up to 3 months. If using in soups or hot meals, simply add from frozen or defrost in the microwave for 1–2 minutes (it defrosts rather quickly).

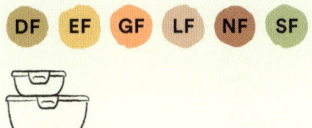

While we are fortunate to live in a time where we can find low-FODMAP stock cubes and ready-made stocks at the supermarket, there is something so satisfying about making a chicken stock from scratch, and it's surprisingly simple to do! All you need is one large pot, a few ingredients and a bit of time for a slow simmer. I like to use the chicken carcass (the bits left over after the meat has been removed), which you should be able to get from your local butcher. If you can't find a carcass, you can use chicken wings or any other bony cuts, but the flavour might not be as rich as with the carcass. Add whatever scraps of vegetables you have on hand, such as carrot, fennel or the green tops of leeks; if you don't have any spring onion (scallion) tops, you can throw in some fresh chives. The main thing is that you simmer the stock low and slow.

Low-FODMAP chicken stock

Prep time: 5 minutes
Cook time: 3 hours
Makes: 4 cups (1 litre)

1 kg (2 lb 4 oz) chicken carcass
200 g (7 oz) carrot, quartered
50 g (1¾ oz) fennel
50 g (1¾ oz) fresh flat-leaf
    (Italian) parsley
3 bay leaves
1 teaspoon whole black
    peppercorns
40 g (1½ oz) spring onion
    (scallion) tops, green parts
    only
2 teaspoons dried or fresh
    rosemary
1 teaspoon dried or fresh thyme
1 teaspoon salt
2 teaspoons apple-cider vinegar
2 teaspoons garlic-infused olive
    oil (optional)

Add all the ingredients to a stockpot and cover with cold water, about 2 cm (¾ in) above the ingredients. Bring to the boil over medium–high heat, discarding any foam that forms on the surface, then reduce the heat to low and simmer gently, uncovered, for 3 hours. If it bubbles too rapidly, it will reduce the liquid too much and the stock will be murky instead of nice and clear, so keep an eye on it and top up the water if needed.

Drain through a sieve or colander into a large bowl or pot to catch all the beautiful stock. Allow the stock to cool slightly before portioning (if not using right away). I find it's easiest to store this in 1 cup (250 ml) quantities.

Store in the fridge for up to 5 days or in portions in the freezer for up to 3 months. If using in soups or hot meals, simply add from frozen or defrost in the microwave for 1–2 minutes (it defrosts rather quickly).

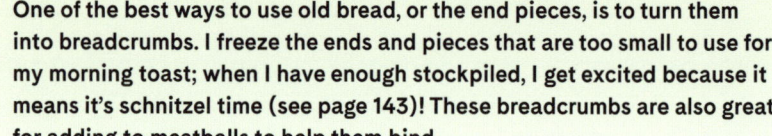

One of the best ways to use old bread, or the end pieces, is to turn them into breadcrumbs. I freeze the ends and pieces that are too small to use for my morning toast; when I have enough stockpiled, I get excited because it means it's schnitzel time (see page 143)! These breadcrumbs are also great for adding to meatballs to help them bind.

Breadcrumbs

Prep time: 5 minutes
Cook time: 10 minutes
Makes: approx. 3 cups (180 g)

200 g (7 oz) day-old bread
   of your choice
1 tablespoon dried parsley
1 tablespoon dried basil
1 teaspoon salt

Preheat the oven or grill (broiler) to 200°C (400°F).

Tear the bread into a blender, then pulse to a coarse crumb. Pour the breadcrumbs into a deep baking tray and mix in the herbs and salt.

Bake in the oven to toast the crumbs for 5–10 minutes, keeping an eye on them and stirring every couple minutes. They can brown very quickly, so keep checking in.

Once the breadcrumbs are light brown, remove from the oven and allow to cool.

Use straight away or store in an airtight container at room temperature for 2–3 weeks.

About the author

Chrissy Glentis is the co-founder and creative mind behind the low-FODMAP food brand Foddies. She has lived with fructose malabsorption and lactose intolerance since the age of 19, and she was sick of eggs on toast being her only option when she went out to eat. Chrissy started Foddies with her husband, Luke, in 2014. Their cafes, offering low-FODMAP dishes, led to a range of packaged products that are available in Australia and the US. Chrissy has been a pioneer in the specialty food space, and has been featured in newspapers and on TV cooking shows for her simple, flavoursome and allergy-friendly dishes. She is based in New Jersey.

Thank you

First and foremost, to my incredible husband, Luke – thank you for your unwavering support, for always being there to encourage me, and for giving me the confidence to take the leap and chase this crazy dream of a career in food. Without your belief in me, none of this would have been possible. We have been through so much together and I am so blessed to have you here with me for this next exciting chapter. I would not be here without you.

To my family, thank you for your patience, love and assistance with recipe testing! Also for chauffeuring me around and making sure I was fed and taken care of during the book shoot.

To our customers and everyone who has supported us through the journey of building our food business, Foddies – you're the heart of it all. Every message, every purchase and your patronage when we had our cafes/restaurants has meant the world and has inspired each page of this book. I truly hope you enjoy cooking these recipes for yourself as much as I have loved cooking them for you over the years.

A huge thank you to my publisher, Melissa, who saw potential in my recipes and believed they were worth sharing. Thank you for taking a chance on me, for pushing this project forward and for convincing your team to let me bring this vision to life.

And to the whole team who made this process not only smooth but genuinely fun and enjoyable – your dedication, creativity and passion have brought this book to life. Working with you all has been a privilege.

Index

Published in 2025 by Murdoch Books, an imprint of Allen & Unwin

Murdoch Books Australia
Cammeraygal Country
83 Alexander Street
Crows Nest NSW 2065
Phone: +61 (0)2 8425 0100
murdochbooks.com.au
info@murdochbooks.com.au

Murdoch Books UK
Ormond House
26–27 Boswell Street
London WC1N 3JZ
Phone: +44 (0) 20 8785 5995
murdochbooks.co.uk
info@murdochbooks.co.uk

For corporate orders and custom publishing, contact our business development team
at salesenquiries@murdochbooks.com.au

Publisher: Melissa Kayser
Editorial manager: Loran McDougall
Design manager: Sarah Odgers
Designer: Vanessa Masci
Editor: Andrea O'Connor @ Asterisk & Octopus
Photographer: Armelle Habib
Stylist: Lee Blaylock
Home economist: Caroline Griffiths
Production manager: Natalie Crouch

Murdoch Books acknowledges the Traditional Owners of the Country on which we live and work. We pay our respects to all Aboriginal and Torres Strait Islander Elders, past and present.

ISBN 978 1 76150 053 4

A catalogue record for this
book is available from the
National Library of Australia

A catalogue record for this book is available from the British Library

Colour reproduction by Splitting Image Colour Studio Pty Ltd, Wantirna, Victoria
Printed by 1010 Printing International Limited, China

OVEN GUIDE: You may find cooking times vary depending on the oven you are using. For fan-forced (convection) ovens, as a general rule, set the oven temperature to 20°C (25–50°F) lower than indicated in the recipe.

TABLESPOON MEASURES: We have used 20 ml (4 teaspoon) tablespoon measures. If you are using a 15 ml (3 teaspoon) tablespoon add an extra teaspoon of the ingredient for each tablespoon specified.

10 9 8 7 6 5 4 3 2 1